HUMAN LOVE—Existential and Mystical

HUMAN LOVE
EXISTENTIAL AND MYSTICAL

by RALPH HARPER

THE JOHNS HOPKINS PRESS
BALTIMORE, MARYLAND

TO MY WIFE

PREFACE

The writer of the Song of Songs said, "Love is as strong as death." If this is true, then love is very strong indeed. Some would go even further and say that love is stronger than death. Let us hope that it is! But apart from death, love is the strongest, whether we think of it as pure passion or as the motive behind all other passions.

There are several loves: inner and outer, centripetal and centrifugal, selfish and unselfish, licit and illicit. And they too are reducible to two fundamental desires: for the creation and for the Creator, or existential and mystical. Mystical love is the love for God, whom we cannot see, and existential love is love for all that we can see, and especially for other human beings.

For some these two loves are opposed. To others the mystical is quite unreal, and the existential is all there is. For still others each love is unsatisfying without the other. The following pages are written from the last point of view, and are intended to define and illustrate the major alternatives that all must choose from sooner or later.

Monkton, Maryland   RALPH HARPER
April, 1966

CONTENTS

HUMAN LOVE—Existential and Mystical

I

1.

THE AMBIGUITY OF LOVE

BETWEEN the existential and the mystical there is an astonishing, sometimes an embarrassing, resemblance. Take for example the line "Sometimes I am so crazed with love that I do not know what I am saying."[1] Who can tell from the words which kind of lover is speaking—existential or mystical? Yet it was St. Teresa of Ávila, and she was most certainly a lover of God, not man. This woman, who described herself as " 'bewildered and intoxicated with love,' "[2] was a mixture of the practical and the sentimental. An extraordinary builder and reformer of convents, she was also perpetually charged with a love of Christ so intense, and so sensually fancied, that it is as impossible to disbelieve in her sincerity as it is difficult to not be made uneasy by the symbols of her infatuation with God. Although she was shrewd in her dealings with the secular as well as the religious, her voices, visions, and levitations make us laugh when they do not exasperate us. But at the very moment we are about to give her up as silly and hysterical, she will recall some vision, like the following, that even though it has an erotic form also has a ring of religious authenticity which can disarm a skeptical reader.

"In his [an angel's] hands I saw a great golden spear, and at the iron tip there appeared to be a point of fire. This he plunged into my heart several times so that it penetrated to my entrails. When he pulled it out, I felt that he took them with it, and left me utterly consumed by the great love of

[1] *The Life of St. Teresa*, trans. J. M. Cohen (Baltimore: Penguin, 1957), p. 281.
[2] *Ibid.*, p. 113.

God. The pain was so severe that it made me utter several moans. The sweetness caused by this intense pain is so extreme that one cannot possibly wish it to cease, nor is one's soul then content with anything but God. This is not a physical but a spiritual pain, though the body has some share in it— even a considerable share. So gentle is this wooing which takes place between God and the soul that if anyone thinks I am lying, I pray God, in His goodness, to grant him some experience of it." [3]

Although her imagery was carnal, the effect on her of this vision was a greater love for God. The wounding— compare St. Francis' more famous stigmata or St. John of the Cross's many mentions of wounds from the touch of God—is not an empty symbol but rather a factual description of the effect of a sudden and intense meeting with the beloved, be he man or God. If it is obvious in such a passage that the imagery is ambiguous, as carnal as it is spiritual, then it is possible that even where the experience itself is unambiguous, the imagery is interchangeable, as appropriate to one kind of love as to another. Evelyn Underhill says as much:

> It was natural and inevitable that the imagery of human love and marriage should have seemed to the mystic the best of all images of his own "fulfillment of life"; his soul's surrender, first to the call, finally to the embrace of Perfect Love. It lay ready to his hand: it was understood of all men: and more-over, it certainly does offer, upon the lower levels, a strangely exact parallel to the sequence of states in which man's spiritual consciousness unfolds itself, and which form the consummation of the mystic life. [4]

We would have no difficulty with "it lay ready to hand," but even if she had not mentioned it, we might have wondered about that "strangely exact parallel to the

[3] *Ibid.*, p. 210.

[4] Evelyn Underhill, *Mysticism* (New York: Meridian Books, 1957), pp. 136–37.

4

sequence of states in which man's spiritual consciousness
unfolds itself." It seems that there is a suggestion here of a
natural interchangeability between the love for man and
the love for God. This does not mean that some mystics
have not deliberately borrowed it—certainly St. John of
the Cross did—or that others, perhaps even St. Teresa of
Ávila, had not completely or successfully sublimated their
sexual desires. It does mean that we would be prudent to
defer judgment on the true home of the imagery. Indeed,
Simone Weil, has claimed, "It is wrong to reproach the
mystics because they use love's language. It is theirs by
right. Others only borrow it."[5] And she too may be wrong
in being so sure that "others only borrow it"; perhaps it is
theirs by right also.

The "sequence of states" to which Evelyn Underhill
calls our attention may be what she elsewhere calls the
three "diagrams or symbolic descriptions of man's in-
ward history," "the three ways in which man's spiritual
consciousness reacts to the touch of Reality," that is,
"the longing for a lost home . . . the craving of heart for
heart . . . the craving for perfection."[6] In the end the three
may be one, or at least parts of the same total experience
of loving. But she may have been thinking rather of the
three stages of spiritual development, which from Dionysius the Areopagite on have been spoken of as purgative,
illuminative, and unitive. And may it not be wise to look
for their analogues in existential experience as well? The
single-minded, obsessive longing of the earthly lover for
his earthly beloved is not unlike the state of recollection,
the stripping for the illumination yet to come, the benev-
olent recognition by the beloved, followed by absence,

[5] Simone Weil, *Waiting for God*, trans. Emma Craufurd (New York:
G. P. Putnam's Sons, 1951), pp. 171–72.
[6] Underhill, *Mysticism*, pp. 126–27.

doubt, suspicion, despair—darkness no less—all preceding the lucky, the unexpected surrender of the absent one to the waiting heart. Who can say that one kind of love is more intense than the other, or, for that matter, more completely developed? The dream is the same, as the following fragment from the medieval manuscript of Beauvais powerfully suggests:

> By day mine eyes, by night my soul desires thee,
> Weary, I lie alone.
> Once in a dream it seemed thou wert beside me;
> O far beyond all dreams, if thou wouldst come![7]

Is the dream of God or of a woman? The words do not tell us. Their very neutrality, their plasticity, suggest that the dreaming state is as important as the figure in the dream.

It is when the dream expresses a longing so heavy it requires carnal imagery to bear its weight that the suspicion arises that suppressed sex has found an outlet. Yet why should we not as easily say that sublimation can sometimes effect a love not only as powerful as a carnal love but completely satisfying? When we read poems like the following it is, in all fairness, hard to doubt that there have been sublimated loves for God that were pure and happy; it is stupid not to acknowledge them with awe. St. Mechthild of Magdeburg's "The Power of Longing" is not a single burst of love from a lonely woman, but a peak in the life of a woman renowned as the soundest German mystic nun of the middle ages.

> Ah, Lord, if only once
> It happened on a day
> That to my heart's desire
> I look on you, and lay
> My arms around you lovingly,

---

[7] *Medieval Latin Lyrics*, trans. Helen Waddell (Baltimore: Penguin, 1952), p. 33.

6

> The rapture of your holy love
> Would flood my soul with ecstasy
> That men have known upon their earthly way.
> And I would suffer after this
> More than the tongues of men can ever say.
> A thousand deaths would be too light,
> I yearn for you so greatly, Lord.
> And wait for you so faithfully.
> If you will suffer me, O Lord,
> I shall pursue and seek you long, in agony.
> For well I know: You, Lord, must be
> The first to feel a want of me.[8]

This is an expression of religious love—mystical—yet what earthly lover would not be moved if he heard his absent love address him in such phrases? In fact, as I know from having looked, it is almost impossible to find carnal love poetry that can match this and other mystical poetry either in intensity or in completeness. But there is more to remark on here. The completeness of St. Mechthild's song resides in her love's being contained between the two extremes of the "If only once" of the first line, and the "You, Lord, must be the first to feel a want of me" of the last lines. The humility at the beginning is taken up into the assurance of the complementary love from the God she has pursued "in agony."

Eight centuries earlier St. Augustine had cried, "Oh, that you would come into my heart,"[9] and only a century before St. Mechthild, tragic Heloise had, seemingly, echoed St. Augustine: "For not with me was my heart, but with thee. But now more than ever, if it be not with thee, it is nowhere. For without thee it cannot anywhere exist."[10] Of course, Heloise was speaking to separated

[8] *The Soul Afire*, ed. H. A. Reinhold (New York: Pantheon, 1944), p. 284.
[9] *Confessions*, trans. Rex Warner (New York: Mentor, 1963), p. 19.
[10] *The Letters of Abelard and Heloise*, trans. C. K. Scott-Moncrieff (New York: Alfred A. Knopf, 1929), p. 60.

Abelard, whom she loved more than God, whereas something in St. Augustine prevented him from loving any human being as he loved God. The similarity of expression, nevertheless, should not be forgotten. It suggests that man, and woman too, is made for a love responsive to desire, and that desire is strengthened by fidelity for the moment when it is rewarded.

Desire is too weak a word to describe the love for God of some mystics. To read of St. Maria Maddalena de' Pazzi's "Loving Madness" is to be shocked, shaken, perhaps convinced.

> She was filled with perpetual fervor. She thought incessantly of God, she spoke incessantly of God, and she wrought for God incessantly. Often it seems as though she had lost her senses and were entirely within God. At times her inner fire was so great that she could not contain it within her breast: it flamed in her face and poured into her actions and words. She, who as a result of penance performed, usually looked weak and feeble, pale and emaciated, grew strong when these flames of love overwhelmed her. Her face became rounder and fervent, her eyes were like two shining stars, and her gaze was serene and joyful like that of a blessed angel. Then she was restless and could not be still. To pour out this fervor she was forced to bestir herself and she was strangely impelled to move about. And so, at such times one saw her moving quickly from place to place. She ran through the convent as if crazed with love, and cried in a loud voice: "Love, love, love!" And since she could not endure this conflagration of love, she said, "O Lord! No more love, no more love!" And she said to the sisters that followed her: "You do not know, beloved sisters, that my Jesus is nothing but love, yes, mad with love. You are mad with love, my Jesus." Once she stripped an image of Jesus of its adornments and said: "For me You shall be naked, O my Jesus, for I cannot endure Your boundless virtues and perfections. I want your naked, naked humanhood."[11]

---

[11] *The Soul Afire*, pp. 286–87.

8

There, you say, it is out at last—the suppressed sexual desire so strong, and so blind, that it finally reaches broad daylight. The fact that this nun was known as a great educator of nuns will hardly quiet the detractors who quiver in outraged modesty at the incriminating words. I said modesty, but it might be just as fair to say a prudery nourished on centuries of Anglo-Saxon puritanism. "You are both God and man," she cried, and for once someone had spelled out the male in Christ. Can we be so sure that the Incarnation did not mean this too? Perhaps it has taken women mystics to see it.

St. Maria Maddalena's "no more love" is a reminder to the rest of us, reflecting in tranquillity and sobriety, that passion may exceed its own tolerance, and not mainly by excess but by contrast with the perfection of the loved one may force the lover to beg for mercy. Few ecstasies are so severe, or, more accurately, so perfectly inspired that they do not wish to be sustained. Usually love suffers a descent after the withdrawal of the loved one; the deflated lover is desolated, abandoned to a world that no longer offers wonders or delights. "How could a man who had once leapt at one bound into Paradise get used to living like everyone else?" And so the life that has been lived in ecstasy, in mystery, turns problematic. There is only one problem left, how to get through the boring days. What a contrast with that period of "loving madness" when reason had been left behind and the soul gave itself with uninhibited concentration to the imagining of the perfections of the beloved. To the world the lover is a ridiculous fool; to the lover paradise is within reach. More than that, as Alain-Fournier once said of himself, "Behind every moment of my life I seek the life of my paradise."

Perhaps a statement like this expresses the meaning as well as the intention of existential love. It is not put in such an exclusively religious manner that we are obliged to assume that behind the existential lies the mystical. "Paradise" may, after all, be only a metaphor to be used interchangeably with existential as well as with mystical, in the same way that the language of human love is borrowed by the mystics. "Perfect," "heaven," "divine" are words used by those who would be the last to claim any first-hand acquaintance with mysticism. Yet it has been said, repeatedly and with conviction in our own un-mystical age, that "in each Thou we address the eternal Thou."[12] To the cynic this looks like having your cake and eating it too. To those still clinging to religion but whose minds are unconvinced by the old terminology, Buber's dialectic has been consoling. We have only to put the declaration as a question, as Sarah Miles does in Graham Greene's *The End of the Affair*, to see that we are dealing with speculation, not settled fact: " 'Was it really You [God] all the time?' "[13] Well, was it?

The question is real and open. Sarah Miles had begun to close it when she asked it; she had been converted away from her adulterous love for Maurice Bendrix and toward an invisible God. She is a fiction, of course, yet people like Sarah have actually lived. Deluded? Perhaps. Frightened? Perhaps. Her lover, Bendrix, certainly thought so. He said, " 'When we get to the end of human beings, we have to delude ourselves into a belief in God.' " No one, not even theologians, would deny that it is possible to delude oneself into a belief in God. There is neurotic, there is hysterical, sick religion, and there is healthy religion. To take the other side for a moment, even delusion is of two kinds, sick and healthy. The mind can make an

[12] Martin Buber, *I and Thou*, trans. Françoise Delisle (New York: Scribner's, 1953), p. 6.
[13] *The End of the Affair* (New York: Viking Press, 1964), p. 150.

Existential and Mystical

honest but bad mistake in appraising reality, without being under compulsion. There is also a kind of delusion, the kind Bendrix had in mind, that grows out of desperation. His way of putting it, " 'when we get to the end of man,' " suggests several possibilities. Most lovers get tired of each other, and of their love; if they are married, and remain married, they keep going by substituting other interests as an insulating wall. Some lovers, like Bendrix, are so suspicious, so unsure of themselves or of those they love, that they deliberately frustrate and end love. And behind these obvious frustrations looms the real threat posed by Greene's sentence, the suggestion that no existential love can be satisfying because sooner or later the finitude of man will be fully experienced and there will be no more to desire.

If, on the other hand, man is a "great abyss"[14] ("There is something of man that the very spirit of man that is in him does not know."[15]) the experience of human finitude can become an experience of infinity as well. So far as observable self-knowledge and knowledge of others goes, it is as fitting to speak of the infinite as of the finite; so it is just as right to amend Greene's sentence by adding: "When we get to the end of the finite, we find the infinite." Is this the same as saying, "We find the eternal Thou, God"? Probably not. We are talking here of the limits of knowing (and they usually involve an "as if," e.g., for all practical purposes "as if infinite"), not the nature of reality. So many pseudo-theological statements turn out to be grounded in psychological intimations rather than in defensible metaphysics. There is no reason to dismiss them entirely for all that. For they show us two things: first, that the human spirit seems to require metaphysical

---

[14] St. Augustine, *Confessions*, p. 84.
[15] *Ibid.*, p. 214.

11

satisfaction, and second, that some psychological experiences are so mysterious that they seem to justify explanations which exceed the strictly descriptive. Such is the character of St. John of the Cross's line, "Then you will give me what you gave me on that other day."[16] We have met this before in St. Augustine, in his experience of the end as the beginning, the new as the familiar. It is an impression, offensive perhaps to logic and common sense, but nonetheless as certain as any sensation or any syllogism. In St. John's mind there is more than pattern and paradox, there is an explanatory cause of the psychological impression, the giver, God. He will give as He has given already. And what He gives, we now realize, is somehow the same thing we were given at some other time. The fusion of cause and pattern, Giver and gift, is typically religious, mystical. And yet it is not difficult to imagine, or remember, the course of human, existential love in which the remembered, absent love becomes present once again, and the dream or first encounter is fulfilled. Indeed, it is precisely this kind of parallel between the existential and the mystical that moves me to consider them side by side.

If the course of love, whether mystical or existential, ends, ideally, in an encounter long desired, it always begins as a search. "By night on my bed I sought him whom my soul loveth."[17] (To this day no one knows for sure whether the love referred to in the Song of Songs is mystical or existential.) "My love is my weight,"[18] said St. Augustine. Perhaps this gravity is sufficient reason for the temptation to believe that God alone fulfills the

[16] *The Spiritual Canticle*, stanza 37, in *The Collected Works of St. John of the Cross*, trans. Kieran Kavanaugh and Otilio Rodriguez (New York: Doubleday, 1964).
[17] Song of Songs, *The Oxford Annotated Bible with Apocrypha*, Revised Standard Version (New York: Oxford University Press, 1965). All biblical quotations are from this edition, unless otherwise noted.
[18] *Confessions*, p. 322.

12

heart's seeking. Men hope for success but they do not always believe in it, and their gratitude when success unexpectedly comes sometimes takes the form of hypothesizing a God. "You were inside me, deeper than the deepest recesses of the heart,"[19] so deep that St. Augustine never even knew God existed, let alone existed in his own errant heart. Then came the conversion, and he did know. As the evangelical hymn has it, " 'He moved my soul to seek Him, seeking me.' "[20] God is the hidden cause. It is not enough to be glad; he must be grateful too. The human soul appraised fundamentally as questing, longing, generates so much power that its extent and intensity astonish. Can all this be mine alone? And here again the temptation arises to hypothesize a self-subsistent Power.

I know no better definition of the soul's desire than that of the Carmelite, Philippe de la Sainte Trinité, " 'To be a person is to be essentially in search of a person.' "[21] We are made for someone else. Even this, however, goes beyond the experience of some men. Take, for example, Dag Hammarskjöld's note in *Markings*: "What I ask for is absurd: that life shall have a meaning. What I strive for is impossible: that my life shall acquire a meaning." Paul Tillich had much to say about the anxiety of meaninglessness, and the quest for meaning, which he thought was the characteristic concern of our century. What kind of meaning? The word itself suggests an answer to a question, and it is hard to avoid thinking that both Tillich and Hammarskjöld, like many others in our time, were thinking of philosophical meanings. And yet sometimes another quest can be felt behind the quest for meaning: we find it

[19] *Ibid.*, p. 60.
[20] Anonymous, quoted in *The Interpreter's Bible* (New York: Abingdon-Cokesbury, 1951–57), V, 112.
[21] Quoted in M. C. D'Arcy, *The Mind and Heart of Love* (London: Faber, 1945), p. 321.

turning up in the very next sentence in Hammarskjöld's *Markings:* "I dare not believe, I do not see how I shall ever be able to believe: that I am not alone." There it is, "that I am not alone." It was this that troubled him. And yet, nine years later, Whitsunday, 1961, when he recorded his own encounter, the ambiguity had not disappeared. "I don't even remember answering. But at some moment I did answer Yes to Someone or Something—and from that hour I was certain that existence is meaningful and that, therefore, my life, in self-surrender, had a goal." The abstractness remained even after the experience of an encounter in which his questioning brought the Challenger out into the open. There was no specific answer, there was not even for sure Someone to say "yes" to. And yet, the very "I don't know Who—what—" indicates the ambiguity that is typical of intimate personal encounters. Put Hammarskjöld's "markings" alongside Lady Julian of Norwich's "I saw him, I sought him; I had him, I wanted him,"[22] and you not only illuminate the former, you may see it as the more human, more poignant converse of St. Augustine's own quest. He sought and he saw; he wanted and he possessed. Lady Julian, who has known more of God's love than any other human, had a different kind of assurance, mixed and more believable, yet tranquil and firm: "I am the ground of thy beseeching. . . . And I will make all things well."[23]

Here are the two authentic notes of religion: the conviction that reality is not a bottomless abyss, and that the ground of being is compassionate. Believe this who can. The believer is not let off lightly but is presented with the bill. As St. Catherine of Siena put it, " 'I require that you should love me with the same love with which I love

[22] *Revelations of Divine Love* (London: Methuen, 1952), p. 22.
[23] *Ibid.*, pp. 89, 62.

14

you.' "[24] We can hear one human lover demanding this of another, loudly, insistently, when love has become one-sided. It should not have to be said at all. But where God is concerned, it has to be said all the time, so much harder is it for man to make the effort to love the invisible God. Harder?—no, it is impossible to conceive a human love which can equal God's. What an impossible love, what an impossible God: yet if man can conceive loving God, not for fear of hell or for hope of heaven, but " 'for thyself alone,' "[25] why should he not be able, helped by God's own unselfish love, to make the ideal reality? This is part of what St. John of the Cross had in mind when he said, " 'He who loves cannot be satisfied if he does not feel that he loves as much as he is loved.' "[26] We want to match the love already offered us, not to lag behind it; and more than that, we want to be loved so much that all the latent love in us can be poured out on a worthy beloved. Yet, in the end, the worthiness of the lover is determined as much by the energy and purity of his own love as by the energy and purity of the one he loves. Unless that other's love precedes, waits, exists, only to respond, love aborts. Perhaps it is such failed love that tyrannizes by demanding to be loved in excess of its own intention to respond. Nowhere in reality is the balance between persons more likely to be misconceived, thwarted, spoiled than in love. Love breeds love, whether human or divine. And love unheard leaves love waiting a bitter "lonely began."[27] The mystic insists God's love can always be heard, if one learns to listen. The existential lover depends less surely on the chance grace of another human being.

[24] *The Soul Afire*, p. 273.
[25] Rābiʻa, the Moslem St. Teresa, *ibid.*, pp. 717–801.
[26] Quoted in D'Arcy, *The Mind and Heart of Love*, p. 329.
[27] Gerard Manley Hopkins, Poem 43, *Poems and Prose of Gerard Manley Hopkins*, selected with an Introduction and Notes by W. H. Gardner (Baltimore: Penguin, 1962). All Hopkins' poems quoted hereafter are from this edition and will be cited only by title or number.

2.

THE EXISTENTIAL

IT is a waste of time to look for a simple meaning of the word "existential" in most books on existentialism; they only add confusion to confusion. I myself am using it in the original, Kierkegaardian sense of an opposite to something: for him it referred to human life as opposed to philosophical abstractions; for me, in defining two loves, it means the passion for creatures as opposed to the mystical passion for the Creator. There are many degrees of caring for reality—for God also—but here I am concerned only with the single-minded obsession with the real that one finds in great lovers, whether of nature or of mankind. In them, with no distractions, no compromises, no hesitations, we can see in love's power and simplicity the central thrust of human nature, out beyond its inner circle of self to the world without which it is incomplete. Self-concern is only part of this primary direction of the developed consciousness.

Existential lovers are those who love other human beings or those who love nature. Usually great lovers are more emphatically of one type than of another. There are exceptions, but they are not the best examples of either type. No one in the nineteenth century exceeds Wordsworth in his uncanny appreciation of the natural world, its beauty and its presence as a consolatory ambience for solitary man. We do not think of Wordsworth also as a great lover of men, or women; we do not go to him to learn of the passions of the human heart. Or take that younger kindred spirit, Francis Kilvert, West country

bachelor parson, whose journals have immortalized country life in the 1870's and whose vivid and spontaneous joys
can be experienced vicariously by readers a century later.
He was a man poignantly in love with each succeeding
night and day, and countless pretty girls as well. But we do
not go to him to learn of love's obsessions or tragedies,
nor do we find in his journals as in Wordsworth's *Prelude* a
speculative effort to locate the destiny of man amid the
sensuous scene. And beyond this, neither Wordsworth nor
Kilvert seems to us to be in love with a reality that can
make a response to the heart's longing for fulfillment.
Wordsworth was a master and a solitary, ministered unto
by sister and friends and admirers. Kilvert loved children
or shy young ladies, who were unattainable because he was
impecunious.

It is only in the poetry of Gerard Manley Hopkins that
for once we can catch the possibility of a love for nature
that is personal in character. His whole being went out to
nature as "the roll, the rise, the carol, the creation,"[1] because, to begin with, he felt, he saw the world "charged
with the grandeur of God,"[2] with "the dearest freshness
deep down things."[3] More than freshness, brooded over
by the Holy Ghost, rather "This piece-bright paling shuts
the spouse/Christ home, Christ and his mother and all his
hallows."[4] And in the poem "Hurrahing in Harvest" he
develops this imaginative theology:

> I walk, I lift up, I lift up heart, eyes,
>   Down all that glory in the heavens to glean our Saviour;
>   And, eyes, heart, what looks, what lips yet gave you a
> Rapturous love's greeting of realer, of rounder replies?

When we add to this poem the one numbered 34, with
its striking claim that "Christ plays in ten thousand places,/

[1] "To R. B."   [2] "God's Grandeur."   [3] *Ibid.*
[4] "The Starlight Night."

18

Lovely in limbs, and lovely in eyes not his," we have in our hands the complete doctrine of the creation as the mystical body of Christ; therefore any part of that creation loved by man can and does respond. This is the imaginative genius of Hopkins, so exceptional that we refer to him only to note that the exception proves the rule.

Since we are drawing a circle around the major types of responsive love, the existential and the mystical, it is only fair that we should concentrate on that love which holds all the strength and all the hope of human nature. It begins with desire for that which it has not had, as does this fragment from the medieval manuscript of Benedictbeuern:

> If she whom I desire would stoop to love me,
> I should look down on Jove;
> If for one night my lady would lie by me,
> And I kiss the mouth I love,
> Then come Death unrelenting,
> With quiet breath consenting,
> I go forth repenting,
> Content, content, content,
> That such delight were ever to me lent.[5]

It is openly sensual, the longing of an embodied spirit. This is human love at its most intense, most concentrated pitch, and therefore it is complete. Let the puritanical and the prurient mumble. This is the heart of human love and mankind believes in it. And when desire is nourished by memory, as in the following line of Petronius Arbiter, another turn is given to the tuning.

> Ah, God, ah God, that night when we two clung
> So close, our hungry lips
> Transfused each into each our hovering souls,
> Mortality's eclipse![6]

---

[5] *The Wandering Scholars*, ed. Helen Waddell (New York: Doubleday, 1955), pp. 223–24.

[6] *Medieval Latin Lyrics*, p. 31.

19

Love not only wants to touch and be touched, but to be "transfused," made one with another. The response wanted is not looks, words, letters, but union. And, untutored, the natural poet in all lovers believes, if only for a moment, in "mortality's eclipse." This was the lifelong personal and metaphysical obsession of Miguel de Unamuno; we love each other so that we will not die utterly: "Only in others can we renew our life and so perpetuate ourselves. Love ever looks and tends to the future, for its work is the work of our perpetuation; the property of love is to hope, and only upon hopes does it nourish itself. . . . Love hopes, hopes ever and never wearies of hoping; and love of God, our faith in God, is, above all, hope in Him. For God dies not, and he who hopes in God shall live for ever. And our fundamental hope, the root and stem of all our hopes, is the hope of eternal life."[7]

Unamuno's over-powering concern with immortality may not be a fair perspective from which to view the intentions of love. For him love is an instrument rather than an end; he would love so that he might live. Others would live so that they might love. And still others would ask only that they might love once before they die.

> Western wind, when will thou blow
> The small rain down can rain?
> Christ, if my love were in my arms
> And I in my bed again.[8]

There is desire, memory, and now in this passage memory and desire combined. One thing only is lacking, the specific ingredient of love that distinguishes it from self-centered desire for possession—humility. In the following passage by Pierre de Regiers, quoted by Simone Weil (of all people) in her *Notebooks*, this note appears.

[7] *The Tragic Sense of Life* (New York: Dover, 1954), p. 199.
[8] "The Lover in Winter Plaineth for the Spring" (sixteenth century), *The Oxford Book of English Verse*, No. 31 (London: Oxford University Press, 1957).

"If once, upon a dark night,
I have placed myself where she disrobes.

I have all the love I can desire;
So if she treats me unkindly,
Whereas another would complain, I remain tranquil . . .

For here I am her lover in secret.

For I do not think I have ever desired anything
But to do to her what might please her.

From far away I am close to her; so true is it
That no one can ever separate friends . . . " [9]

This younger contemporary of Abelard and Heloise, the canon Pierre de Regiers, writes as Launcelot and other courtly lovers imagined. Remember C. S. Lewis' summary of courtly love: humility, courtesy, adultery, and religion of love.[10] Nowhere is it clearer than in courtly love—and the Malory legends are excellent illustrations—that love is evoked by beauty, and love pleads for beauty's response. This is what humility bows before: humility, that preparatory omen of the spiritual in the carnal. The most single-minded, obsessional passion gathers up in itself the whole world and sees the world as if for the first time with new eyes. It is not one beauty that is loved, but all.

When my arms wrap you round I press
My heart upon the loveliness
That has long faded from the world.[11]

These lines by Yeats elevate our understanding of love from phenomenology to aesthetics, and from there the path is short to metaphysics. Beauty is the order and perfection of all that is real for man.

[9] *The Notebooks of Simone Weil*, trans. Arthur Wills (London: Routledge and Kegan Paul, 1956), II, 638–39.
[10] *The Allegory of Love* (New York: Oxford University Press, 1958), p. 12.
[11] William Butler Yeats, *The Collected Poems* (London: Macmillan, 1957), p. 69.

3.

THE MYSTICAL

WHO HAS understood the mystical better than St. Augustine? And who has been more afraid of what he understood? A crypto-Manichee to the end of his life, this strange and great man was drawn to God by beauty. "In my ugliness I plunged into the beauties that you have made. . . . Those outer beauties kept me far from you, yet if they had not been in you, they would not have existed at all. . . . Late I loved you, beauty so ancient and so new."[1] Here we have the beginning of that fifteen hundred years or more of irreconcilable opposition between Beauty and beauties, between God and woman. In order to explain what I mean by "mystical" I must put aside the sensual, the carnal, and speak of the love of God as if between each man and God there were nothing but man's tragically mistaken disposition to be side-tracked from the major quest of his life, the quest for God. We recall that pathetic little plaint of St. Augustine (as paraphrased by Meister Eckhart): "Lord, I did not want to lose you, but I did want to own some creatures besides you. It was because of my greed that I lost you—for it did not please you that anyone should own creatures that are false and at the same time own you who are the truth."[2]

Are creatures false because they are creatures? This is the temptation behind Manicheism and the puritanism from

[1] St. Augustine, *Confessions*, p. 235.
[2] "The Book of Divine Consolation," *Meister Eckhart, Selected Treatises and Sermons*, trans. James M. Clark and John V. Skinner (London: Faber, 1958), p. 115. This is a free rendering by Eckhart of a passage in Bk. X, ch. 41 of the *Confessions:* "I, in my covetousness, while not wanting to lose you, wanted at the same time to possess a lie."

23

which we ourselves are only now trying to escape. It was only a half step, it seems, from St. Paul's exhortations to mortify the flesh, to monasticism's contempt for the flesh. "Despise! despise! despise!" Yet this very flesh, female flesh, conceived of the Holy Spirit, produced a carnal Christ. To read the well-known spiritual works of Eastern and Western Christianity, one would never know the Incarnation had any significance for man. Thomas à Kempis' *The Imitation of Christ* is typical of this dualism: "When you love creatures, that love deceives you and never stays the same; when you love Jesus, your love is loyal and lasts. The man who clings to anything created will fall together with that fallible creature; if he holds fast to Jesus he will stay firm for ever."[3] This sounds like the sour notes of a disappointed lover. Can it truly be said of all loves that they end in deception? Thomas goes further and urges his disciples to "despise everything else"[4] for God's sake. It is hard to see how God would be served, even if other loves had failed. Before he is through he asks, "What greater freedom is there than to desire nothing upon earth?"[5] This is worthy of Buddhism but should not be part of a Christian theology. It is almost unbelievable that so much of the spiritual life of Christendom has been vitiated by this sort of thing. Spirit is spirit, and flesh is flesh, and never the twain shall meet. But if there is any theological truth unique to Christianity it is that the two did meet, and so that they may yet meet more profoundly.

The manuals for religious are filled with such lines as, "Oh God, I want thee, and I do not want anything else."[6] And laymen have echoed such sentiments in hymn singing.

[3] *The Imitation of Christ*, trans. Ronald Knox and Michael Oakley (New York: Sheed and Ward, 1965), p. 69.
[4] *Ibid.*, p. 100.
[5] *Ibid.*, p. 130.
[6] *Letters of Dom John Chapman* (London: Sheed and Ward, 1959), p. 289.

Existential and Mystical

Most of them can hardly have known—let alone meant—
what they sang. Fortunately, hymns are sung because of
their tunes not because of their words. But even if ordinary
people were half-persuaded, and some have been, to desire
God alone and be indifferent to the rest of creation, they
would at least be in good company. Their betters, like
St. Thomas Aquinas, had long ago settled that "man's
ultimate happiness consists in contemplation."[7] In the
Summa Contra Gentiles St. Thomas lists the many things that
man's happiness does not consist of: carnal pleasures,
honors, wealth, worldly power, even the moral virtues and
faith in God. It did not occur to him that some might
think they could find their happiness, and in this life too,
with each other in marriage. The writings of the "saints"
bear a eunuch's bias which is so noticeable that only
ecclesiastical habits of obedience on the part of married
people could have prevented them all these centuries from
crying, "Perverse!"

Unfortunately, the damage has been done, and its effects
are insidious. To see this as clearly as possible, look for a
moment at the arguments St. Augustine uses—they are
typical of Christian asceticism: "The love of God, the love
of our neighbor, is called charity; the love of the world,
the love of this life is called concupiscence."[8] "Not that
the creature ought not to be loved; but if that love is
referred to the Creator, then it will not be desire but
charity."[9] What about the love of a man for a woman?
St. Augustine, like St. Paul before him, finding it difficult
to separate lust from sexual love, preferred all men to be
celibates like himself. "Our body too might be said to be a
prison, not because it is a prison which God hath made,

[7] *Summa Contra Gentiles*, Bk. III, ch. 37.
[8] *An Augustine Synthesis*, ed. E. Przywara (New York: Harper and Row,
1958), p. 341.
[9] *Ibid.*, p. 346.

but because it is under punishment and liable to death."[10]
The trap has been set, sprung, and the victim caught.
Henceforth, mistrusting God's creation, its sex, its desire,
passion, mutual love, and loving fidelity, the ascetics will
lay down the rule, "Better marry than burn,"[11] but don't
marry unless you have to. The challenge was thrown
down—the body is a prison—and it took the "wandering
scholars" and the apostles of courtly love to try to meet it.
They lost out in the end.

As fierce as St. Augustine, St. Bernard six centuries
later provided the argument that was to hold up longer,
into modern times. In arguing that "the hunger of man's
heart cannot be satisfied with earthly things,"[12] he pointed
out that "nowhere is there any final satisfaction, because
nothing can be defined as absolutely best or highest"[13] but
God. This could have settled the question, if only it were
true that "nowhere is there any final satisfaction." Philosophers can be bemused by their universals. The fact that
every man and woman is not only mortal, but imperfect in
various ways—and that God is both eternal and perfect—
does not mean that all men cannot find final satisfaction
in earthly things. There is plenty of evidence that some
men do and that they do not feel anything significant
would be added if they loved God also, let alone despised
their earthly loves for the sake of God. It never seems to
have occurred to St. Bernard—and consequently one
should not expect him to make any literal sense of the Song
of Songs—that some men find God even though their love
for God's creatures and that this might be the Christian and
the biblical thing to do. Lest I leave the impression that

[10] *Ibid.*, p. 1.

[11] I Corinthians 7:89.

[12] St. Bernard of Clairvaux, *On Loving God* (London: SCM [Student Christian Movement] Press, 1959), p. 35.

[13] *Ibid.*, p. 37.

Existential and Mystical

only Western ascetics talked like St. Augustine and St. Bernard, I should mention St. Simeon the New Theologian (*sic!*), who said: "A heart is and is called pure when it finds in itself no worldly thought, but wholly cleaves to God, and is so united with Him that it no longer remembers anything worldly, either sad or joyful, but remains in contemplation. . . ."[14] There are no geographical boundaries to asceticism.

When mysticism is not tainted by a Manichean asceticism, however, the authentic craving for eternity and presence cannot be ignored. Rābi'a, the Moslem St. Teresa, is free from this: " 'O my God, my concern and my desire in this world, is that I should remember thee above all things of this world, and in the next that out of all who are in that world, I should meet with thee alone.' "[15] Free of contempt, her longing is as legitimate as the exclusive longing of one earthly lover to be with another. For there are men and women with an insatiable craving for God, and as Blessed John Ruysbroeck put it, " 'If God gave to such a man all the gifts which all the saints possess, and all that He is able to give, but without giving Himself, the craving desire of the spirit would remain hungry and unsatisfied.' "[16] And we ought not to laugh even when the imagery of the craving strikes us as unreal. Richard Rolle's "Song of Love" might well have been written by St. Teresa, so human and direct is the language of love. Its purity and credibility are, in part, due to Rolle's relative indifference to the type of contemptuous asceticism championed by St. Bernard.

> My song is a sighing, my life is spent in longing for
> the sight of my King, so fair in His brightness.

---

[14] *Writings from the Philokalia* (London: Faber, 1957), p. 137.

[15] Underhill, *Mysticism*, p. 248.

[16] Rābi'a, *ibid.*, p. 265.

> So fair in Thy beauty! Lead me to Thy light, and feed me on
>   thy love! Make me to grow swiftly in love and be Thou
>   Thyself my prize.
> When wilt Thou come, Jesus my joy, to save me from care and
>   give Thyself to me, that I may see Thee evermore?
> Could I but come to Thee, all my desires were fulfilled. I
>   seek nothing but Thee alone, who art all my desire.[17]

If human life is thought of in terms of a quest, whether for
heaven or for earth, it is just as true of the mystical way as
of the existential that there can be differences in the desired
end. Albert Camus commented on one of these when he
said, "At certain moments everything yearns for that spiritual home. 'Yes, we must go back there—there, indeed.'
Is there anything odd in finding on earth that union that
Plotinus longed for?"[18] Elsewhere he spoke of "the landscape
of Plotinus, a nostalgia for a lost paradise."[19] Camus' own
vision of happiness, like that of Plotinus, was of a rational
unity impossible in the modern world, and unlike Plotinus
he longed for human justice and—a different order—the
North African sun and sea. If, as Evelyn Underhill has
said, "mysticism is seen to be a highly specialized form
of that search for reality, for heightened and completed
life,"[20] then an intellectual vision such as that experienced
by Plato, Plotinus, and St. Augustine himself might well
fulfill the longings of a certain type of mind. It might even
be called "a secret knowledge of God," something both
Christian and Platonist fervently want.

Yet, for the Platonist, "it is not that the Supreme reaches
out to us seeking our communion; we reach toward the
Supreme; it is we that become present."[21] For the Christian
it is the other way around. God becomes present to us,

---

[17] *The Soul Afire*, p. 267.
[18] "Summer in Algiers," *The Myth of Sisyphus* (New York: Alfred A. Knopf, 1955), pp. 151–52.
[19] *The Myth of Sisyphus*, p. 131.
[20] *Mysticism*, p. 93.
[21] Plotinus, *The Enneads* VI. 33–36.

having moved us, his creatures, to move towards him. Joseph Maréchal, whose work on the psychology of mystics is to be trusted, summarized by claiming that "the fundamental mystical phenomenon is the feeling of God's presence."[22] He would be the first to add that for a Christian it is not primarily an experience of tranquillity or even, according to Wordsworth again, "a presence that disturbs,"[23] but a presence that responds. A more recent, and no less authoritative, student of Christian mysticism, David Knowles, simply states that "all genuine mysticism [he is speaking only of Christian mysticism] is the direct action of God bestowing knowledge and love of himself."[24] And this is the sense I myself would give to the word "mystical" as opposed to "existential." It is the experience of God's grace, not merely His being, that makes the common ground with carnal love.

St. Augustine's epigram "You are the love by which the soul loves you" could be applied to carnal love, marriage, as appropriately as to the love for God. If "pure contemplation consists in receiving,"[25] carnal love is raised to respectability by unswerving compassion. The pattern of true love is interchangeable, from mystical to existential, from existential to mystical, as one can see perhaps from this passage from Walter Hilton: "We do right nought but suffer Him and assent to Him; for that is the most we do, that we assent wilfully to his gracious working in us. And yet is that will not of us, but of His making; so that me thinketh that he doeth in us all that is well done, and yet we see it not."[26] A good love is surprised at being loved at all; and it is being loved that makes it good.

[22] *Studies in the Psychology of the Mystics*, trans. Algar Thorold (London: Burns Oates and Washbourne, 1927), p. 102.

[23] "Tintern Abbey."

[24] *The English Mystical Tradition* (London: Burns and Oates, 1961), p. 134.

[25] St. John of the Cross, *The Living Flame of Love*, stanza 3, paragraph 36, in *The Collected Works of St. John of the Cross*, p. 624.

[26] *The Ladder of Perfection*, Bk. II, ch. 34 (Baltimore: Penguin, 1957).

4.

THE TWO PLEADINGS

EVERYONE must decide for himself what love is. His conclusions will depend as much on himself as on his good or bad fortune, and they will be marked by the age in which he lives, as we are all to some extent creatures of our time. When it is conventional to disbelieve in unselfish love, ideas about the possessiveness of love will flourish and tales of unselfish love will be ignored. When it is conventional to believe in unselfish love, some men will at least make some effort to be unselfish. "Give me one that longs, and he will understand what I have to say," said St. Augustine. This cuts both ways, of course—longs to possess, or longs to give? We do understand best what we have begun to experience, and we begin along with the examples of those around us. There are always exceptions, and in the end it is the exceptions who become the spokesmen and the living documents to be taken seriously. The issue is never whether a man can love, but whether he can give as well as take, whether he can leave himself for a moment for the sake of another. Proust—and now Sartre—denied this. "The bonds that unite another person to ourselves exist only in our minds. Memory as it grows fainter relaxes them, and notwithstanding the illusion by which we would fain be cheated and with which, out of love, friendship, politeness, deference, duty, we cheat other people, we exist alone. Man is the creature that cannot emerge from himself, that knows his fellows only in himself; when he asserts the contrary, he is lying."[1]

[1] Marcel Proust, *The Sweet Cheat Gone*, ch. 1, *Remembrance of Things Past*, trans. C. K. Scott-Moncrieff (New York: Random House, 1932).

31

No greater challenge to our reading of our own experience, and of our honesty, has ever been laid down. And we cannot dispose of Proust's conviction, tempted as we may be by its pathos, by explaining it only as the product of homosexuality. There are many people who do not, who do not seem to want to, emerge from themselves, or who want to and apparently cannot. If their lot is not universally prescribed, then something has gone terribly wrong for them. And they would not be able to understand, except perhaps by desire, either the existential or the mystical as loves inspired by love and empowered to give in return. If love has any meaning for them it might be "shadows of desires," or, in the words of the fourteenth-century poem "Quia Amore Langueo,"

> In a valley of this restless mind
> I sought in mountain and in mead,
> Trusting a true love for to find.[2]

Trusting, but always doomed to be disappointed, either by its own greed for possession or the voraciousness of others.

This restless craze to possess defines for many people the term "erotic." Much of the discussion of "two loves," *eros* and *agape*, has been prejudiced by the assumption that there is a fundamental dichotomy between a possessive love, which is easy to find in everyone, and an unselfish love, which is much harder to achieve. I almost said, "harder to find," but that is not true; whether it is generosity or a true reading of the lives of others, it is much easier to see unselfishness in others than in ourselves. We do not even have to fall back on the comparatively remote figures of Christ and some of the saints; we can observe examples of unselfishness in our own surroundings. Pity the man or

[2] *The Oxford Book of English Verse*, No. 29, ed. Arthur Quiller-Couch (New York: Oxford University Press, 1957).

32

woman who has not been brought up in such a family or community (or church). He will assume that love is basically possessive, self-centered, and he will point to many instances of the destructive nature of its obscure force.

The exponents of the theory of the two loves—*eros* and *agape*—make much of the wide difference between *eros* as *animus*, *agape* as *anima*, *eros* as typical of the intellect's intention to comprehend at any cost, even to truth, *agape* as the will's wish to give and belong. The centripetal *eros* underlines the concern man has with all that is essential to human nature; the centrifugal *agape* cares only for the existence, the being of man and God, leaving their nature to be understood in their own terms and in their own time. Compared to *eros*, *agape* is relaxed. *Eros*, compared to *agape*, is energetic, fervid. In addition, *eros* has usually been associated with the visible world, the earth and sex, *agape* with the invisible, God, and, by derivation, the saints. Both *eros* and *agape* want a response, however different: *eros* wants to be allowed to have its way, *agape* wants to be welcomed with open arms.

Of all those who have considered the nature of love no one has understood the complexities and dialectic more subtly than Martin D'Arcy. His book *The Mind and Heart of Love* would seem to have said the last word. He is not satisfied with a theory of love that disjoins *eros* and *agape* utterly, holding that *eros* too must include the best in human nature, that "*eros* should stand for both the ecstatic, irrational and self-effacing mood of love, and the rational, self-assertive and possessive form, as they are found in human experience." He defines *agape* as "God's special love and man's response to it as inspirited and energized by it," and in his own view, which is an extension of the mystical view that man loves because he is loved, *agape* is the heart of *eros* the mind. D'Arcy's dialectic is based on a passage from an essay by Pierre Rousselot in which the two loves, the existential and the essential, are seen in this intimate relationship: "In so far as it translates the sensible given into a something, into essence, the soul is desiring itself and wishes to realize itself as humanity; in so far as it affirms that being exists, it wishes to realize itself as being and desires God. These two loves are not external to one another; the love of God is internal to the love of self; it is its soul. And it is the source of our intellectual vision. If the soul is sympathetic to being as such, it is because it is capable of God."[3]

And so we come to understand the mystical love as the cause of the existential love, erotic love now being admittedly both selfish and unselfish. If this is so, then we can go one step further than D'Arcy went. We can say that whenever love is centrifugal, it is *agape*, whether it is existential (of creatures) or mystical (of God). It is the *agape* within the *eros* that finally frees *eros* from the prison of self. And *eros* is born of the refusal of *agape*. *Eros* is a corruption of *agape*. As D'Arcy says, "We aspire to be loved by one whose love breaks down the last reserve of the self, so that we can belong utterly to him."[4] And although he had God in mind, why is it not just as proper to think this of man, or woman? In most people's experience of the breaking down of reserves of the self, it is done by some other human being rather than, in any observable, distinct way, by God.

This may suggest the validity of courtly love, "the religion of love," which Malory's Launcelot and Gwynevere played

[3] "Métaphysique thomiste et critique de la connaissance," *Revue néoscolastique de philosophie*, Nov., 1910, pp. 476–509.
[4] *The Mind and Heart of Love*, p. 325.

34

out to the finish. Their love ended in tragedy: their exposure before Arthur, the end of the Fellowship of the Round Table, that brave and noble attempt at a social order with charity as its motive, and the bitter deaths of Arthur and of themselves. There were too many conflicts to be borne, the marriage bond between king and queen, adulterously broken, the fealty of Launcelot to him "that was the moste kynge and nobelyst knyght of the worlde," the moral requirements of the quest of the Grail, and the malice of Sir Mordred and Sir Aggravayne. In the end there could be only disaster, death, and renunciation: " 'I fully understand for the first time how I had betrayed them and brought each to his death through my selfish love and pride.' "[5] But his friend Sir Ector saw him differently: " 'A, Launcelot . . . thou were hede of al Crysten knyghtes . . . and thou were the trewest lover of a synful man that ever loved woman, and thou were the kyndest man that ever strake wyth swerde.' "[6] Malory's *Morte D'Arthur* leaves nothing out. We find in it the erotic and the contemplative, adulterous love and the quest for the Holy Grail, a noble king and a court torn between a new social ideal and a sacramental vision. For a time everything existed side by side. But the weight of all these loves was too heavy, and without a better understanding of love, of God, of woman, of the realm, of sacrament, it all had to fall apart. But while it lasted it was good. As Richard Rolle said of love in general, so we might say of Malory's world: "A reasonable soul cannot be without love while it is in this life . . . for to love and to be loved is the secret business of all human life. . . . If therefore you seek to be loved, love; for love demands a

---

[5] *Le Morte d'Arthur*, a new rendition by Keith Baines (New York: Mentor Classics, 1962), p. 506.
[6] *The Works of Thomas Malory*, ed. Eugène Vinaver (London: Oxford University Press, 1959), p. 882.

return."[7] Adultery aside, all this can be seen in the exclusive passion which Launcelot and Gywnevere had for each other, for in spite of his errands and her jealousy it is their love for each other that must be adjudged authentic, and not the arranged marriage between king and queen.

Courtly love was an attempt outside the law to retain the spontaneity and permanence of sexual love. The conviction behind it—"This alone is real"—and its submission to superior law when the chips were down form an interesting comparison with contemporary attitudes. I would submit as an illustration the frenzied shouting of Meursault at the end of Camus' *The Stranger*; when holding by the throat the prison chaplain who had offered the usual consolations, he tells him that "none of his certainties was worth one strand of a woman's hair." His defiance, however, sets him apart from Launcelot, who could not escape the judgment of his time (and ours) that however real and true his love for Gwynevere, it was adulterous and wrong. But Meursault is right in a way. As Etienne Gilson has said, a real philosopher always speaks of things; it is the professors of philosophy who talk of ideas.[8] Would that this were true, or at least that there were many real philosophers. The only ones I can think of, defined this way, are Augustine, Pascal, and Kierkegaard, and several existentialist successors in our century (and I doubt that Gilson, the Thomist, had them in mind).

Gilson has a point, however, that we would do well to take seriously. The pursuit of truth needs more than professional skillfulness, more certainly than the skill of those biased by temperament to analyze words and sift arguments. It needs above all men who are moved by their

---

[7] *The Fire of Love* in *English Writings of Richard Rolle*, ch. 25, ed. H. E. Allen (London: Oxford University Press, 1931).

[8] *The Philosopher and Theology* (New York: Random House, 1962).

love of what is real to understand it and themselves. It needs also, for its own protection, freedom to examine and, if necessary, to discard both conventions and laws that freeze the quest for and the enjoyment of ultimate reality, whether that be existential or mystical. Nothing that is real, nothing that is true, should ever be excluded from the philosopher's life or the philosopher's theories. Absolute dichotomies, such as between *eros* and *agape*, earth and heaven, man and God, are just such forms of exclusion that warped or weary men fashion to further narrow ends. "Nothing is true," I repeat after Camus, "that forces one to exclude."[9]

The notion of heaven—of Spirit generally—has been presented in such a way that it evokes only a sense of intense emptiness and a choking homesickness for its opposite, earth. So Emily Brontë's Cathy Earnshaw felt: " 'If I were in heaven, Nelly, I should be extremely miserable. . . . I was only going to say that heaven did not seem to be my home, and I broke my heart with weeping to come back to earth; and the angels were so angry that they flung me out into the middle of the heath on the top of Wuthering Heights, where I woke sobbing for joy.' " Yet this same Cathy, sick, disspirited, torn between two kinds of lovers, one gentle, the other passionate, later longed for the heaven that she earlier rejected. And so many others, waiting until "the busy world is hushed, and the fever of life is over, and our work is done,"[10] can accept with anticipatory gladness a heaven that excludes earth. There are good reasons in our lives why some of us should welcome earth to the exclusion of an unreal heaven, or heaven to the exclusion of an unsatisfactory earth. But then some of us should not try to be philosophers. Whether

---

[9] "Return to Tipasa," *The Myth of Sisyphus*, p. 198.
[10] *The Book of Common Prayer*, p. 594.

we are threatened with exclusion from earth or from heaven, from man or from God, an equitable judgment would agree rather with the sentiment of Francis Thompson's line, "Yet was I sore adread, lest, having Him, I must have nought beside."[11]

This is the tension between heaven and earth that our late and beloved contemporary, Dietrich Bonhoeffer, had in mind when he said, "I have long had a special affection for the season between Easter and Ascension Day. Here is another great tension. How can men endure earthly tensions if they know nothing of the tension between earth and heaven?"[12] This tension between the existential and the mystical is what George Fox meant by the two pleadings:" 'I found that there were two thirsts in me: the one after the creatures to get help and strength there; and the other after the Lord, the Creator. It was so with me . . . that there seemed to be two pleadings in me.' "[13] The two pleadings represent, with neither one suppressed, the full range of human love. We are made to experience, and therefore to want, the visible and also the invisible, the carnal, and also the spiritual, the secular, and also the religious, the natural and the profane, and also the super-natural and the religious, the creation and also the Creator. Turning one's head away from something does not make it unreal; Teilhard de Chardin has said,

> Either the Christian will repress his taste for the tangible and force himself to center his interest on purely religious objects only, trying to live in a world made divine by the exclusion of the largest possible number of worldly objects; or else, harassed by that inward conflict which hampers him, he will dismiss the evangelical counsels and decide to lead what

---

[11] *The Hound of Heaven*, No. 333, in *The Oxford Book of Christian Verse* (London: Oxford University Press, 1951).

[12] *Letters and Papers from Prison* (London: Fontana, 1959), p. 87.

[13] Underhill, *Mysticism*, p. 178.

38

seems to him a complete and human life; or else, again and
this is the most usual case, he will give up any attempt to
understand: he will never belong wholly to God, nor ever
wholly to things; imperfect in his own eyes, and insecure in
the eyes of men, he will become resigned to leading a double
life. I am speaking from experience.[14]

He could have mentioned two other options. Just as the
ascetic Christian is taught to repress his taste for the tangible, so the worldly man (who often thinks of himself also
as a Christian) excludes God from any serious part in his
life. And to many God has become only an empty word.
Finally, we should be able to ask by now whether in order
to be honest one must lead a double life; is it not possible—
only theoretically, naturally—that we might belong to God
wholly by belonging to things wholly?

Another man's way of putting the dilemma—or the
double thrust—is William Lynch's: "We wish on the one
hand to grasp meaning to the full, so that there is no pain
of questioning left; on the other hand we have an equal
longing for pure, unalloyed concrete objects, and for not
having to go beyond them to get at meaning, joy, or
illumination. This double longing exists in all of us. We
want the unlimited and the dream, and we also want the
earth."[15] The double longing does exist; nobody can
sensibly deny it. And the longing for the unlimited and the
dream is one way of talking about God without mentioning his name. Father Lynch would wish to add, I am sure,
that it is only when man comes to the end of the finite that
he finds the infinite. How else, I would agree, can we do so
unless we have plunged into the tangible earth? Exactly
so, and the spiritual writings that make us most uncomfortable are precisely those that seem to have come out of
an attempt to bypass the embodied life that is ours by

[14] *The Divine Milieu* (New York: Harper and Row, 1960), p. 20.
[15] *Christ and Apollo* (New York: Sheed and Ward, 1960), p. 15.

right and opportunity. Hans Kestranek says this very well when he writes of homesickness:

> "Much has been said about a homesickness for the hereafter; a genuine homesickness is only possible if we do not stifle an earthly homesickness on hearing its voice. We dream, build into the heavens, and neglect to lay the foundation. We speak of this life, as the Way; however, it should be a golden threshold of the gate to Paradise. Here too, God holds sway, and can there be limits to eternity? Here too is eternity. . . . One world of the present and the hereafter, therefore also one belief for both, one kingdom of God, therefore also one kingdom of God also on earth as well."[16]

But we are going too fast. The existential and the mystical have been separate options for many centuries, and there is more than one way of understanding their relationship. Some have thought them different but equally real (St. Francis, Malory, Hopkins). Some have thought them so different as to be incompatible (St. Bernard, the ascetic tradition in general), with the mystical superior to the existential. Others, especially in our century, would define them separately but would consider the existential alone real, and the mystical imaginary. And these would also suggest that the mystics have sublimated the real for the sake of the imaginary. Others see them as equally real, but the existential as explicit, the mystical as implicit (Buber, Simone Weil, D'Arcy). And some others would not wish to define the relationship but would be satisfied with a variety of symbolic representations of the double longing, from the controversial Songs of Songs to the more ambiguous use of the symbols of love and quest in St. John of the Cross and Alain-Fournier's *The Wanderer*. In St. John's poems the imagery of human love (the imagery, in fact, of the Song of Songs) is deliberately used to ex-

[16] Quoted by Friedrich Heer in "The Saint of a New Era," *Cross Currents*, Fall, 1955, p. 317.

press man's love for God and God's love for man. In *The Wanderer* the fictional world not only keeps alive an autobiographical experience but can be read as a paradigm of man's quest for paradise.

We must be wary of neat schemes into which we put favorite writers and antipathetic points of view. Not everyone will fit into these combinations of affirmation and rejection, not even when we speak of double affirmation, or the symbolic affirmations which leave the theoretical decisions open. I am reminded, particularly by Rilke's insistence on the one hand and some difficulties in explaining Emily Brontë's understanding of passion on the other, that to speak of affirmation and rejection so firmly is to forget that some loves are, so far as one can tell, simply nontransitive. They do not have objects. I call such loves metaphysical, to distinguish them from the existential and the mystical, which do have objects, different objects. And so there are transitive and non-transitive loves, as well as inclusive and exclusive loves, single loves, double loves. We must not confuse one with another.

On the other hand, why should we assume a priori that there is no underlying unity or fusion? Conflicts between the existential and the mystical usually arise when people, for a variety of reasons, are more inclined to love in one direction rather than in another. Some are more naturally sexual than others; some are more naturally religious than others. Neither disposition should be allowed to pass judgment on the other. And in all fairness, I should add, some people dislike taking sides, even when sides should be taken. When a similarity of behavior and expression appears, there is good reason to look for a common phenomenology of the spirit. Objects of love aside, when love is considered intransitively, without another person on the far side of desire, the desire itself is still worth considering. And if it looks much the same as the desire for man, and the desire for man as the desire for God, a significant unity of experience may be assumed. There are it seems, three kinds of unity which can be applied to our understanding of love: psychological unity (it *feels* the same), intentional unity (it *means* the same in some way, as implicit-explicit), and unity of being (it *is* the same). Generally, the two loves are kept separate in intention. Heloise loved Abelard, not God. St. Bernard loved God and hated Abelard. There are easy rules of thumb for distinguishing the existential from the mystical. Now she thinks and dreams of her lover; now she prays in the chapel to God. Launcelot goes to bed with Gwynevere; later he goes looking for the Holy Grail in wayside chapels. There is no unity of experience here. And there is no psychological unity either, at any rate for Heloise or St. Bernard. Neither one knew the opposite kind of love. Launcelot's divided self is another matter.

When all the distinctions have been carefully made and considered, the fact remains that they are being made about love, and love is one. This is not to settle the question by fiat. Of course love is love—who would deny it? But when we recall that love itself needs to be defined and explained, no matter which kind of love we are talking about, we then realize that we have only begun to explore the main centrifugal thrust of the human spirit. It is so easy to be indifferent, or to hate. What gives us the interest and the energy to love? Where does love come from? Is it sentimental to suggest that it is hardly ours to give? It is that difficult much of the time. And further, what is it all about? I mean not what or whom do we want, but for what? What is man made for that he must love, in one way or another, one kind of reality or another, even imaginary reality? These aspects of love justify our referring to a unity in being. Love is one; it is men who are different.

42

II

5.

NON-TRANSITIVE LOVE

WHERE love is concerned we can always begin again. Men have made too many assumptions of hard and fast oppositions. It is not only possible that some of them are wrong, it is certain. Fate and the human temperament have conspired to bias, and in the skillful hands of a St. Bernard or a St. Augustine bias has the force of truth for weaker minds. And when backed up by the totalitarian authority of ecclesiastical tradition and establishment bias even looks holy. Today rebellion is still soiled and soured by enslavement and doubt. Or worse, many minds are for all practical purposes incapable of imagining either God or love of God. And when that happens, when *agape* disappears as a human option, it is liable to survive only in an uncertain, corrupted form in *eros*. I am thinking of the curious attitude that love is only our struggle to possess a stranger who is trying also to possess us, an attitude expressed by Sartre and others admittedly indifferent to religious questions. A world without the possibility of response is a world completely outside the mystical tradition. It is outside the existential as well.

We must "learn to see," said Rilke, for it is certain that we have not understood love rightly:

> Is it possible that one has not yet seen, known and said anything real or important? Yes, it is possible.
> Is it possible that despite discoveries and progress, despite culture, religion and world-wisdom, one has remained on the surface of life? Yes, it is possible.
> Is it possible that the whole history of the world has been misunderstood? Yes, it is possible.

45

Is it possible to believe one could have a God without using him?

Yes, it is possible.[1]

More than that, this is certain too. God is not being used as much in our time as in the days of the mystics. Is it possible that we have God all the same? Yes, even *eros*, corrupted *eros*, needs a hidden *agape*, a hidden God to survive at all. Richard Rolle had something to say about this: "I dare not say that all love is good, for that love that is more delighted in creatures than in the Maker of all things, and sets the lust of earthly beauty before ghostly fairness, is ill and to be hated; for it turns from eternal love and turns to temporal that cannot last. Yet peradventure it shall be the less punished; for it desires and joys more to love and to be loved than to defile and be defiled."[2] In Dostoevsky's *Crime and Punishment* there is a fine example of this in the figure of Svidrigailov, the sad sensualist who wanted to be loved so much by Dounia Razumihin that he would not take her when he had her. Rilke may have had something like this in mind, but something else as well. He was convinced that for a while it would be better for all of us if we tried to do without God altogether, until we are ready for the kind of love he has to give. As he put it, "We sense that God is too difficult for us."[3] Rilke meant what Tillich called "the God above gods." Our gods are too small for that God. And we can now see the relevance of this statement by Bonhoeffer, a more engaged witness: "God is teaching us that we must live as men who can get along very well without him. The God who is with us is the God who forsakes us. The God who makes us live in this world

---

[1] *The Notebooks of Malte Laurids Brigge*, trans. M. D. Herter Norton (New York: Capricorn Books, 1958), pp. 28–30.

[2] *The Fire of Love* (London: Methuen, 1914), pp. 79–80.

[3] Rilke, *Notebooks*, p. 159.

46

without using him as a working hypothesis is the God before whom we are ever standing."[4]

Rilke's gloss on this would probably be that we have to get along without God because we do not know any more what he is anyway. Our expectations have been betrayed and we are best left alone. No one has written more plausibly of man in his loneliness than Rilke: the loneliness of the child, afraid of the "night without objects," "the Big Thing," and death—always death, "a death of one's own." "I have learned to be afraid with real fear, fear that increases only when the force that engenders it increases. We have no idea of this force, except in our fear . . . and yet it is our own force. . . . We no longer recognize that which is our own and are terrified by its extreme greatness."[5] Perhaps this is where a man should begin if he wants to understand love, begin with that force Rilke talks about, which is probably that frail, penetrating sword of the spirit that can be shattered so easily and yet point the way to heaven itself, if rightly used. It is the life force that G. B. Shaw liked to write of, yet changed in an instant this life force becomes death itself.

Rilke's view of this force was that its real name is love, a love so pure that no suffering should be avoided in order to keep it free. His pages in *The Notebooks of Malte Laurids Brigge* about several little-known women is important not as commentary on their writings, but for the convictions of Rilke himself.[6] Of Bettina von Arnim, the girl who fell in love with the elderly Goethe and wrote him love letters, Rilke asks, "How is it possible that everyone does not still speak of your love? What has since happened that was more remarkable? You yourself knew the worth of your love; you recited it aloud to your greatest poet, so

[4] *Letters and Papers from Prison*, p. 122.   [5] Rilke, *Notebooks*, p. 145.
[6] *Ibid.*, pp. 174–203.

that he should make it human. . . . But perhaps it will some-
day appear that here lay the limit of his greatness. This
lover was imposed upon him, and he was not equal to her.
What does it signify that he could not respond? Such
love needs no response."[7] I am not sure that Bettina really
cared whether Goethe responded or not. Apparently, she
continued to write letters to him after his death. Perhaps
also his failure to be moved by her love does indicate some
limit to his greatness. That may be argued. But Rilke's
claim that Bettina's love needed no response is worth
examining. If she had wanted a response, or wanted to
possess and be possessed, Rilke's statement would make
no sense. Assuming that she did not care, that her love
was pure, indifferent to reward, we could understand it.
Yet, even so, conditioned somehow to think of love in
terms of response, we do find it difficult to sympathize
fully with her. Bettina herself said something that Rilke
might have held to be a justification: "Perhaps God through
the Beloved penetrates into our heart . . . what have we in
our heart but only God—And if there we did not feel him,
how and where should we seek his trace?"[8] If this makes
sense, then it was not Goethe whom Bettina loved, but
God through Goethe. And so it would make no difference
whether Goethe responded or not. "The woman who loves
always transcends the man she loves, because life is greater
than fate. Her devotion wants to be immeasurable; that is
her happiness."[9]

Unfortunately our loving is restricted by those we love
(it would be more accurate to say "love through"), particularly by the convention that love is to possess and be possessed. There is no security in that. On the contrary,

[7] *Ibid.*, p. 175.
[8] Bettina von Arnim, *The Diary of a Child* (Berlin: Trowitzsch and Son, 1839), p. 98.
[9] Rilke, *Notebooks*, p. 176.

48

security in love lies in the loneliness of the lovers who "hurl themselves after him they have lost, but even with their first steps they overtake him, and before them is only God."[10] The true lover goes through the finite, to the end, and then beyond. Does this mean that the lover uses his beloved? I fear that for Rilke it did. And it is possible that his persuasion about pure love may have been prompted by a peculiar personality warped from childhood. Who can tell? And for us it does not matter. There is still something important enough in his view of love to justify our looking at it.

In his meditation on Sappho, Rilke says that people have seen "only excess, not the new unit of measure for love and heart's distress," the power to love without return.[11] Who is equal to such a love? Only God. "She knew that nothing can be meant by union save increased loneliness; when she broke through the temporal aim of sex with its infinite purpose; when in the darkness of embracing she delved not for satisfaction but for longing."[12] The longing for the infinite which is at the heart of love, even of sexual love as the romantics understood so well, is constantly being thwarted by the apparent aim of love, especially of sex, to possess. Then satisfaction allows us to forget longing. If love could survive satisfaction, it would be the equivalent of the love of God.

Of such love Abelone, beautiful Abelone, sang in the moving third stanza of the anonymous German song:

"You make me alone. Only you can I interchange.
A while it is you, then again it is a murmuring,
or it is a fragrance with no trace.
Alas, in my arms I have lost them all,
Only you, you are born always again:
because I never held you close, I hold you forever."[13]

---

[10] *Ibid.*, p. 198.   [11] *Ibid.*, p. 202.   [12] *Ibid.*, p. 203.
[13] *Ibid.*, p. 208.

Is this love at a distance, or love thwarted of satisfaction, or love not wanting possession? Is it real love at all? Abelone's beloved is real enough to have a certain effect on his lover, to keep her love alive. Abelone had "yearned to remove from her love all that was transitive, but could her truthful heart be deceived about God's being only a direction of love, not an object of love? Didn't she know that she need fear no return from him? Didn't she know the restraint of this superior beloved, who quietly defers delight in order to let us, slow as we are, accomplish our whole heart? Or did she want to avoid Christ? Did she fear to be delayed by him halfway, and by this to become beloved?"[14] And then we read the marginal notes Rilke had added: "To be loved means to be consumed. To love is to give light with inexhaustible oil."[15] Is this what is best for man, to be given the freedom to accomplish his whole heart, to be encouraged to let all the love in him flow out? And it is God alone who knows how to defer delight so that this can be done? Correction—not "knows how to," but "can."

And finally Rilke re-tells the story of the Prodigal Son, the man who left home because he "did not want to be loved."[16] (How different from St. Maria Maddalena de' Pazzi's " 'No more love, no more love.' " Her breathless love was to suffocation, she could not stand it, it stretched her tight beyond toleration.) The Prodigal Son, as Rilke saw him, was only a boy who had been smothered, passively, by the love of his family. This happens and some do run away to be free of possessive love. Others ought to. But few know that "profound indifference of the heart" which to Rilke was indistinguishable from the desire to penetrate the beloved without consuming. Likewise the Prodigal Son, in his version, "intended never to love, in

<hr />

[14] *Ibid.*, pp. 208–9.   [15] *Ibid.*, p. 209.   [16] *Ibid.*, p. 210.

50

order not to put anyone in the terrible position of being loved."[17] But he learned little by little to love without possessing. And after a while "he could weep for nights then with yearning to be himself penetrated by such rays."[18] And it is as if Rilke were saying, here is the real tragedy of love: that a man or woman should "desire infinitely to possess," and yet be subject to the "terror lest anyone should respond."[19]

There is also the comedy of Stendhalian success in love— "Is that all it is?" And, beneath that, there is the discovery that the beloved is unworthy, banal, stupid, or vicious. Rilke aimed much higher. He feared to be enveloped by compassion, a love which says, "Don't worry, you are so safe in our arms, you don't even need to love any more." He insisted on distinguishing between a love that consumes and a love that cuts through like a laser beam. He believed that it was possible for man to discipline himself to love in the latter way. His new asceticism of love even allowed at a certain stage for the revival of a longing to be loved, once the mind had dispossessed itself of the wrong manner of loving and being loved: "His life . . . began its long love to God, that silent, aimless labor. For over him, who had wanted to withhold himself for always, there came once more the growing and undeviating urge of his heart. And this time he hoped to be answered. He longed to be loved at last in so masterly a way, his senses, accustomed to far distances, grasped the extreme remoteness of God."[20] The Prodigal Son worked so hard at learning to love that he "almost forgot God." He remembered his childhood back home, with everything left unfinished when he had gone away. And so he returned—not having heard Thomas Wolfe's wise warning, "You can't go home." He went

---

[17] *Ibid.*, p. 212.   [18] *Ibid.*   [19] *Ibid.*, p. 213.
[20] *Ibid.*, p. 214.

home. And he was seen, recognized, and forgiven. This is what spoiled it, the forgiveness that enveloped him just as love had threatened to smother him before he ran away: "What did they know of him? He was now terribly difficult to love, and he felt that One alone was able for the task. But He was not yet willing." [21] He had returned to a world where he did not belong, to people who could not understand the crushing burden of their kind of love. But he was not yet ready for the "penetrating radiance" of God. Or was it that God was not ready? Rilke's second loneliness is far worse than the first. The first comes from an awareness of the life force that seeks expression before it dies. The second comes from a desperate desire for a love that is not yet ready to meet one half way. If this is evidence of God's departure or his non-existence, Rilke does not say. His silence encourages us, however, to wonder whether God's unwillingness to meet man when man thinks he is ready for God is not a discreet testimony of God's grace, free to descend and penetrate in His own good time.

[21] *Ibid.*, p. 216.

6.

CONFLICT BETWEEN THE
EXISTENTIAL AND THE MYSTICAL

THE MOST remarkable thing about the story of Heloise and Abelard is that it really happened. Had it been fiction or a legend, it might still be the classical example of an irreconcilable clash between the existential and the mystical. With all the elements that make for scandal, it is nevertheless worthy of study by the most sober of philosophical historians.[1] It began with seduction and continued along a course marked by marriage, castration, conventual immurement, and ended in a common grave. These two were the most renowned of their time even before they met, Heloise at eighteen the most learned woman in France, and Abelard the most popular teacher in all Europe.

Brought to him for tutoring, Heloise was marked by Abelard almost at once as fair game: "Seeing in her, therefore, all those things which are wont to attract lovers, I thought it suitable to join her with myself in love, and believed that I could effect this most easily. For such renown had I then, and so excelled in grace of youth [he was thirty-nine] and form, that I feared no refusal from whatever woman I might deem worthy of my love."[2] Abelard, a tonsured clerk—not yet ordained—had never been in love before. His vanity stands out, even years later, in his own recounting of the affair. So much that it is tempting to disbelieve him when he writes of "being wholly inflamed

---

[1] See, for instance, Etienne Gilson's *Heloise and Abelard*, trans. L. K. Shook (Ann Arbor, Mich.: Ann Arbor Paperbacks, 1960).

[2] *The Letters of Abelard and Heloise* p. 11.

with love for this girl." But believe it we must, for it was certainly an inseparable ingredient in what very rapidly became his passion for her. "And so, our books lying open before us, more words of love rose to our lips than of literature, kisses were more frequent than speech. . . . No stage of love was omitted by us in our cupidity . . . the less experienced we were in these joys, the more ardently we persisted in them and the less satiety did they bring us."[3]

He neglected his studies, his lectures becoming repetitions of what he had already given. His pupils saw the difference at once, and while they were bored by his teaching they were made jubilant by the songs he wrote for Heloise, songs which were soon sung all over Europe. The letters he wrote to Heloise in those days are now lost, but some of the songs perhaps survive in the collections of medieval Latin lyrics. Almost from the beginning the affair was known to everyone except Heloise's uncle Fulbert; when he discovered them, the fateful drama unrolled with measured beat. Abelard tried to silence Fulbert by marrying Heloise secretly after their child Astrolabe had been born. Heloise had objected strongly to the marriage and tried to dissuade him with arguments drawn from classical and Christian writings. She held that a married philosopher would look ridiculous and that it should be the aim of them both to preserve his fame. She was only reminding him of what he too had once taken for granted.

> For what concord is there between pupils and serving-maids, desks and cradles, books or tablets and distaves, styles or pens and spindles? Who, either, intent upon sacred or philosophic meditations can endure the wailing of children, the lullabies of the nurses soothing them, the tumultuous mob of the household, male as well as female? Who, moreover, will have strength to tolerate the foul and incessant squalor of babies? The rich, you will say, can, whose palaces or ample abodes

[3] *Ibid.*, p. 13.

contain retreats, of which their opulence does not feel the cost
nor is it tormented by daily worries. But the condition of
philosophers is not, I say, as that of the rich, nor do those who
seek wealth or involve themselves in secular cares devote
themselves to divine or philosophic duties.[4]

To tell the truth, they were equally obsessed with their
fame, she as well as he. Abelard said, "She asked me what
glory she was like to have from me when she made me
inglorious and equally humiliated herself and me."[5] He,
judging the situation differently, resolved to marry her so
that he "might suffer no loss of reputation thereby."[6]
Always the more timid of the two, he was soon proved
wrong. If we are tempted by their excessive concern for
their fame to think their love a product of vanity alone—or
concupiscence, to use one of Abelard's favorite words—
we should remember that he was capable of saying later:
"Each grieved most, not for himself, but for the other.
Each sought to allay, not his own sufferings, but those of
the one he loved."[7] And yet the first thing he did when he
recovered his health after his castration was to make sure
that Heloise took the veil, obviously so that no one else
could enjoy her. Only then did he become a monk, and
later a priest and abbot. Shadows of Launcelot and Gwynevere up to this point, they became quite different afterwards. For a time Abelard visited Heloise often, until
absurd scandal obliged them to part for ever. Several years
after their separation Heloise saw a copy of the history
of their "calamities," as Abelard called it, that he wrote in
the form of a letter to someone else, and her reply was the
beginning of a short but, on her side, fevered correspond-
ence that has no rival. The burden of this was, to sum it
up in an epigram from the *Anthologia Latina*, "Still let me
love, though I may not possess."

[4]*Ibid.*, p. 17.   [5]*Ibid.*, p. 15.   [6]*Ibid.*   [7]*Ibid.*, p. 14

55

The letters reveal a conflict as wide as the seas, between a woman whose "unbounded love" could not be killed even by the priggishness of a man who had all along one thing in the forefront of his mind, to protect his reputation. The love was existential, transitive—no doubt of that—yet if there was ever a real Abelone her name was Heloise. Her love persisted beyond the unworthiness—or, more accurately, the unresponsiveness—of its object: "It is thou alone that canst make me sad, canst make me joyful or canst comfort me. . . . Nothing have I ever required of thee save thyself, desiring thee purely, not what was thine."[8] One thing perhaps she did require, and did receive—to be linked to his name forever. Yet it is he who is now linked to her love, she being the more original of the two. Preferring "love to wedlock, freedom to a bond,"[9] the name of concubine or whore to wife, his strumpet than an empress, she tried to shock him into returning words of love. She got nothing but mealy-mouthed homilies, hardly worthy of the leading philosopher of the twelfth century. Angered by his apparent indifference to her she told him that "concupiscence joined thee to me rather than affection, the ardour of desire rather than love."[10] He could not agree more: "He [Christ] truly loved thee, and not I. My love, which involved each of us in sin is to be called concupiscence, not love."[11] He may have been right, at that. Perhaps her unbounded love was much the same as that *agape* of which Christ was the model and the medium for this medieval affair. Her summary of her feelings could be the model for *agape* at any time. "For not with me was my heart, but with thee. But now, more than ever, if it be not with thee, it is nowhere. . . . While with thee I enjoyed carnal pleasures, many were uncertain whether I did so from love or from desire. But

---

[8] *Ibid.*, p. 57.   [9] *Ibid.*   [10] *Ibid.*, p. 59.
[11] *Ibid.*, p. 103.

now the end shows in what spirit I began."[12] She was thoroughly human, and on the whole as honest as she could be. Is it her state of having been abandoned by Abelard, forced into a profession which she had not sought, that accounts for occasional notes of hysteria? Like Abelard himself she seems to enjoy recounting the scandal of their pleasures—he calls them obscenities—and the notoriety of their affair. Unlike him she adamantly refuses to turn her love for him toward God. It is natural to conclude that after his castration Abelard's shame made it easy for him to dampen his own ardor, particularly if it was based for the most part, as he always claimed, on lust. Her love, on the other hand, survived this obstacle, and driven on by dreams and memories she loved him as passionately as before.

> So sweet to me were those delights of lovers which we enjoyed in common that they cannot either displease me nor hardly pass from my memory. Whithersoever I turn, always they bring themselves before my eyes with the desire for them. Nor even when I am asleep do they spare me their illusions. In the very solemnities of the Mass, when prayer ought to be more pure, the obscure phantoms of those delights so thoroughly captivate my wretched soul to themselves that I pay heed to their vileness rather than to my prayers. And when I ought to lament for what I have done I sigh rather for what I have had to forego. Not only the things that we did, but the places also and the times in which we did them are so fixed with thee in my mind that in the same times and places I re-enact them all with thee, nor even when I am asleep have I any rest from them. At times by the very motions of my body the thoughts of my mind are disclosed, nor can I restrain the utterance of unguarded words.[13]

Not since Sappho had a woman spoken of sexual love with the directness that men think is reserved for men. The more she mortified the flesh, the more her mind wanted to

---

[12] *Ibid.*, p. 60.　　[13] *Ibid*, p 81.

sin, the more she burned with "old desires." She had become a nun at nineteen, after one of the most ardent affairs of all time; is it any wonder that she could not turn off her desire so soon? The wonder is that she was never able to turn it off.

And so the scandal of their love remained, but in a new form. Like Abbot Abelard, Abbess Heloise became famous for her piety. As Abelard wrote, "All alike marvelled at her religious zeal, her good judgment, and the sweetness of her incomparable patience in all things."[14] She knew better. "They preach that I am chaste who have not discovered the hypocrite in me. They make the purity of the flesh into a virtue, when it is a virtue not of the body but of the mind. I am judged religious at this time, in which but a little part of religion is not hypocrisy."[15] All the while she was charging God with the cruelty that had torn Abelard from her, and at the very moment when their love had been purified by the sacrament of marriage. It is fascinating to contemplate this woman's desperate defiance of God, not only from the bosom of a convent but from the scrupulous, and apparently completely convincing, observance of a religious life involving the direction of souls. Remembering that this is a medieval woman, and therefore one incapable of the modern escape hatch of atheism, we now are considering one who could not for a moment suppose that God was not a living God, creator, redeemer, and judge. God for Heloise was as real as Abelard, but not as lovable. Her complaints were more obstinate than Job's. Unlike him, she never retracted: "In the whole period of my life I have ever feared to offend thee rather than God, I seek to please thee more than Him. Thy command brought me, not the love of God, to the habit of religion. See how unhappy a life I must lead, more wretched than all others;

[14] *Ibid.*, p. 41.   [15] *Ibid.*, p. 82.

58

if I endure all these things here in vain having no hope of reward in the future. For a long time thou, like many others, hast been deceived by my simulation, so as to mistake hypocrisy for religion."[16] Is this the last word, her own judgment on herself? It could be. Yet, although she defied God more brazenly than Job, she also loved more. Like "the woman in the city which was a sinner"[17] who washed the feet of Jesus with tears, she had loved much. In any case, as Henry Adams pointed out, "She was worth a dozen Abelards, if only because she called St. Bernard a false apostle."[18] That intractable enemy of Heloise and Abelard, that apostle of divine love, was finally put in his place by Abelard's friend, Peter the Venerable. Peter wrote to Bernard, " 'You perform all the difficult religious duties; you fast, you watch, you suffer; but you will not endure the easy ones—you do not love.' "[19]

But it is Abelard of whom we must speak last. Heloise was indeed worth a dozen Abelards; we need not bring St. Bernard into it in order to say that. We may be amused at the confusion of piety and commonsense even in Etienne Gilson's commentary on their affair, but truth must be rescued in the end. On the one hand Gilson says (is it only lip service to religion?), "When all is said and done, it is Abelard who is right," or, "Heloise was the first of many romantic heroines driven into evil by love."[20] We only need to hear Abelard's final summary of their disastrous affair as having been ordained by God, "as though He were reserving us for some great ends,"[21] to laugh away such attempts at whitewashing. Gilson himself does

---

[16] *Ibid.*
[17] St. Luke 7:37.
[18] *Mont-Saint-Michel and Chartres* (New York: Doubleday, 1959), p. 321.
[19] *Ibid.*, p. 352.
[20] *Heloise and Abelard*, p. 65.
[21] *The Letters of Abelard and Heloise*, p. 99.

better than that. He says, "Perhaps she was far closer to
divine charity than many others who dethrone God for a
great deal less than Abelard, or who do not even so much
as recall what is the greatest and the first commandment.[22]
If this seems to be as much a question as a conclusion, we
may guess which it is by reading on. "Her problem is to
find in the passion this man inspires the strength required
for a life of sacrifice which is both meaningless and impossible save on the level of the love of God."[23] It is possible
to imagine an abbess performing her religious duties both
scrupulously and without sincerity, possible but not usual.
Nothing about Heloise was usual. It is hard, however, to
avoid the force of her reputation for irreproachable sincerity.
The modern mind prefers neat solutions, even neat conflicts. Heloise perhaps does not fit ready-made categories.
I do not mean that she loved God more than she knew,
but rather that there was more divine love in her than she
knew. I mean more—that this alone would account for her
undying love for Abelard and her willingness to defy an
image of God presented to her as a foe of their love. Once
again, it is Peter the Venerable who put his finger on the
truth. When Abelard died, he wrote Heloise a letter which
is a model for all letters of condolence. Peter had loved
them both, and admired Heloise from the beginning.
" 'My affection for you does not begin today, but dates
from a long way back. I was scarcely more than a boy,
hardly a young man, when the renown, not yet of your
religious life, but of your noble and praiseworthy studies
reached me.' "[24] And so he prepared her heart to hear him
out. " 'Venerable Sister, he to whom you were joined
first in the flesh and then by the stronger and more perfect
bond of divine charity, he with whom and under whom
you too have served the Saviour, is now sheltered in the

---

[22] *Heloise and Abelard*, p. 96.   [23] *Ibid.*   [24] *Ibid.*, p. 119.

bosom of Christ. Christ now protects him in your place, indeed as a second you, and will restore him to you on that day when He returns from the heavens between the voice of the archangel and the sounding trumpet.' "[25] Christ, "the second you," Christ, the second Heloise, will restore Abelard to Heloise. Is it worth it? Is Abelard worthy of Heloise? How easy it is to condemn him out of hand. And I would do so were it not for a poem written by Abelard at the very time that he was telling Heloise to forget him, the one command from him she could not obey. It is his "David's Lament for Jonathan."

> Low in thy grave with thee
> Happy to lie,
> Since there's no greater thing left love to do;
> And to live after thee
> Is but to die,
> For with but half a soul what can life do?
>
> So share thy victory,
> Or else thy grave,
> Either to rescue thee, or with thee lie:
> Ending that life for thee,
> That thou didst save,
> So Death that sundereth might bring more nigh.
>
> Peace, O my stricken lute!
> Thy strings are sleeping.
> Would that my heart could still
> Its bitter weeping![26]

Can anyone believe Peter Abelard was not thinking of Heloise when he wrote this? And so can anyone now believe that he did not continue to love her, in his way, as much as she loved him in hers? The conflict between the existential and the mystical here is a conflict between fornication and fame, not between sex and religion. The castration of Abelard was the fixative that preserved the picture.

[25] *Ibid.*, p. 121.   [26] *Medieval Latin Lyrics*, p. 181.

Religion was not yet ready for undying human love, the very love that found its strength and conviction in some place that defied scandal and all the later efforts to comprehend. If *agape* is more than a word, it should be applied to both Heloise and Abelard whose existential love had a secret mystical source.

7.

IDENTITY OF HUMAN AND DIVINE

To speak of any love as an affair is to imply that it has a beginning and an end, and is not everlasting. Defined in this way, many marriages should be called affairs. And many affairs start off with the naïve assumption that, without marriage, they can last forever. Love is what we make of ourselves with each other. Neither Heloise nor Abelard had any illusions from the start as to the nature of their liaison; neither expected marriage to change anything. But as we look back at them, it may appear that they understood less than they imagined. There was no end to their affair. Except for the fact that the liaison was destroyed by Abelard's castration, it did not even have the principal hallmarks of a liaison, the deep insecurity and mistrust that sooner or later characterize most love affairs.

In Graham Greene's *The End of the Affair*, Maurice Bendrix, a bachelor and a novelist, falls in love with Sarah Miles, wife of a civil servant, and she with him. From the beginning their love is both passionate and furtive. By temperament he is twisted, bitter, mistrustful of self, and envious of others; she is trustful and capable of giving herself unreservedly. Greene loads the scale in such a way that their love is doomed from the start. Even her love could not heal him. He carries his habits of anxiety, jealousy, insecurity, and hate right into their love; the need to be cautious, on the one hand, and her tranquillity, on the other, combine to transform his desire into suspicion. How the affair would have ended naturally we need not guess because Greene contrives (surely this is the word) to drop a bomb on the house in which the two are making love one afternoon, and Sarah, supposing that her lover is dead (Greene leaves us in doubt), promises a God she has not believed in up to that time that she will give up Bendrix if he is restored to life. Bendrix then rises from the floor, and the affair is over.

And so what conscience in adultery could not do, a *bomba ex machina* does do. Of course, this undercuts to some extent the universal relevance—to say nothing of the plausibility—of Sarah's firm renunciation of her lover. Even though we are told that his desire had become more like hatred than love, that they had both "begun to look beyond love," and that "love had turned into a love affair,"[1] who can say how or whether it would have ended? But perhaps Greene is in the right after all. In spite of his haste to get to the point of his novel, he might have remembered that affairs are ended usually, not by conscience, but from the outside. What is harder to believe is that Sarah should keep her vow. Nevertheless, we are meant to look at a love so strong that it could encompass both the existential and the mystical. For not even renunciation of the affair dampens her love for Bendrix. " 'I want ordinary corrupt human love. . . . This is the end, but dear God, what shall I do with this desire to love? . . . Did I ever love Maurice as much before I loved You?' "[2]

We are asked to imagine a woman with an enormous capacity for love—a saint. And this saint begins her progress in sanctity by loving a twisted human being. When she discovers the reality of God, she gives up the human being, although not her desire for him. Ignorant of God, innocent of guile, living with a husband who does not know how to tap the reserves of her love, she comes to life and to belief, but only in time to leave the problems of

---

[1] *The End of the Affair*, p. 39.   [2] *Ibid.*, p. 152.

loving creatures to those who are left after her early (and must we not again say contrived and timely?) death. Bendrix and the husband are left to take care of each other, and Bendrix begins his own more natural journey out of hate and disbelief toward God.

The main question running through the novel is not whether an affair has an end but whether human love is the same as an affair and therefore must end. Does the author really believe in human love except as something to "squander," so that man can come to the end of himself and begin to love God (or, as Bendrix in his bitterness suggests, delude himself into believing in God)? I am not sure. He is very eloquent about the squandering: " 'You were there, teaching us to squander, like You taught the rich man, so that one day we might have nothing left except this love of You. But You are too good to me. When I ask You for pain, You give me peace.' "[3] He gave no peace, however, to Bendrix, "one of misery's graduates." But then Bendrix did not have the good fortune to be born whole and trustful, or to have been baptized a Catholic when a child. There is, no matter how one puts it, a certain determinism about the characterizations, which undermines plausibility and makes it easy for the novelist to solve inherently difficult problems.

Sarah Miles had a vision of love that would seem to have surpassed Greene's contrivances: " 'Love doesn't end. Just because we don't see each other. . . . People go on loving God, don't they, all their lives, without seeing him? . . . That's not our kind of love. . . . I sometimes don't believe there's any other kind.' "[4] When she made her vow over what she took to be his dead body, " 'I'll give him up forever, only let him be alive with a chance,' " she said once more, this time only to herself, " 'People can love without

---

[3] *Ibid.*, p. 109.   [4] *Ibid.*, p. 82.

seeing each other, can't they, they love You all their lives without seeing You.' "[5] For many people this is the real difficulty about belief; they cannot see the God in whom they are asked to believe, let alone love. Yet to turn the problem around, how many do go on loving those they no longer see, whether because of separation by society, conscience, distance, or death?

How is this possible? Love of the absent is too real to be denied or to be explained away as a trick of memory. Why does not human desire always give up when frustrated? Beyond Sarah's vision is her answer, or at least the suggestion of an answer, "the hint of an explanation": " 'Did I ever love Maurice as much before I loved You? Or was it really You I loved all the time? Did I touch You when I touched him? Could I have touched You if I hadn't touched him first, touched him as I never touched Henry, anybody? And he loved me and touched me as he never did with any other woman. But was it me he loved, or You? . . . For he gave me so much love and I gave him so much love that soon there wasn't anything left when we'd finished but You.' "[6] What does Greene mean by her loving Maurice "more"? Can love of the absent be more intense than love of the present? It can, if the love had been moderate before. But this is not the test case that he offers us. Sarah and Maurice loved each other so much they had begun to burn their love up. It is more likely that Sarah's subsequent love was of a different kind, full of compassion as well as desire, and that ambivalent pity which elsewhere in Greene's canon is the cause of tragedy rather than the vehicle of healing grace.

Sarah begins to wonder whether all along she had not been loving God. Only God, and only apparently Maurice? Or God along with Maurice? The difference is important.

[5] *Ibid.*, p. 117.   [6] *Ibid.*, p. 150.

Was Maurice only a cover for God? Was Sarah, was God, just using poor lame Maurice in order to convert her soul to God? Or, a third possibility, was her love for God there all the time as an enabling love, enabling her to love Maurice? Only those present can be touched. And she also wonders whether she was not always touching a present God when she touched the present Maurice. If Maurice was present, why not God, even if He could not be seen? Did touching Maurice enable her to touch God? Is this the way to God—not the way to look at Him, or to pray to Him from afar, not even to love from the distance—the way to stand in the presence of God? Indeed, is it the only way?

And what about Maurice, bitter, jealous man, hating God with a hate as real as love—or was it the other side of love, the side known only to self-mistrust? Did Maurice, desiring Sarah's body, love her at all? Or was he too loving God through her, struggling despite himself to depart from hate into God's presence? Did he love only God all the time, and is that why he came to the end of love, because he no longer needed it once he was near enough to God for God to take over? Were these two human beings using each other, or using each other up? Is this the meaning of human love? We must use each other up, and so we arrive at God? Or, as Bendrix suggested in his pain, do we arrive at the end of ourselves only to fool ourselves into imagining God?

Greene suggests that when their affair was over there was only God left to love, and that that is the way it must be. But even he permits them both to go on loving each other —desiring each other even—in their separation. We may ask at this point why they had to be separated at all, and why we have to assume that human love comes to an end before death. Is the answer simple after all, that Greene felt adultery cannot be condoned? Is it that simple? But why should he have set the story up that way in the first place, why an adulterous love? We might say, because he likes scandal. But what does that mean? Why should he? A scandalous love, whether a real one, as between Heloise and Abelard, or this fictional one, can provide tests for the quality and range of love. If it does not do that, the love is too trivial to bother with. These two stories, Heloise's and Sarah's, are not trivial. Each is carried to the place where we onlookers are forced to ask ourselves anew whether we really understand what is going on when two human beings smash their lives—and sometimes other people's lives as well—in a love that excludes everything in the world except themselves.

Put this way, love would have to be redefined as an intensity of selfishness that is doomed to get what it deserves, its own extinction. Yet there may be, even in such an affair, now and then another element that explains, even if it cannot justify, the ecstasy and the pain. For what we are seeking is an explanation of a desire so intense that it goes to the end of man. Graham Greene's story would be trivial and meaningless if his lovers were not the kind of human beings who cannot be satisfied with resentment (Bendrix) or peace (Sarah). Both want to understand themselves and what they are doing when they love. And neither can understand himself without supposing a third. This much we can read with sympathy. My own reservation begins and ends with my wish that Greene had asked us to look at two lovers who, despite the things that can separate —and in real life there are more than he has mentioned— not only learn to love God in each other, but learn to love each other in God.

The question, of course, must be asked, is this just a manner of speaking peculiar to theologians? If there is no

God, anything said about him is nonsense. And if there is a God, a good many assertions are just as nonsensical. How can anything be loved in anything else? Is this possible? Indeed it is. We can love ourselves in other people, the way a parent all too often loves his own image in his child. This is the love of the projected self. We can love another person because he reminds us of someone else, his parent perhaps. This is love by analogy. We can love something in a person which has not yet come out. This is a love of the future. We can love that in a person which does not yet and perhaps never can exist. This is a love of wishful thinking or mistaken identity. And finally, and to the point, we can love that in another that is struggling to exceed the bounds of his finitude. We are what we are, but what we struggle to understand and to accomplish always exceeds what we already know and have done. We do not belong entirely to ourselves, but to the future and to the unborn creation of our vision and our love.

When we love that vision and love in someone else, we are in love with something greater than he is, and which he has not yet become. That is what it means to say we love God in someone else and, similarly, in our mutual love for each other. This is why lovers experience a sense of mystery beyond their understanding, not only in the gift to each other of love, but in the reaching out of love itself. And not only in sexual love or family love, not only in friendship either, but in the larger range of love within the social and political order. The common efforts to bring about the unity of men, through political and ecclesiastical institutions, the struggles to eliminate poverty and prejudice, elevate the feelings of those who want and those who care. And it is this elevation of sentiment that requires special terminology reserved by theologians for divinity: "Did not thy father do judgment and justice? Then it was

69

well with him. He judged the cause of the poor and needy; then it was well. Was not this to know me? saith the Lord."[7] This is how the Bible understands God, in the experience of active compassion. So much of the difficulty that modern men, untouched by biblical ways of thought, have in believing in God is that like the young Augustine they try to conceive God as a spiritual substance—a metaphysical object of some kind—and when they fail, give up. The biblical attitude is quite different. It is concerned primarily with action and history, and apart from pointing out those acts which need to be radically distinguished from other acts, with the help of a symbolic terminology the biblical mind does not need metaphysics. The speculative theologian takes up where the speculative historian and moralist leave off. Unfortunately, the average person listens to the speculations of the theologians rather than to the historian or moralist.

Once we begin to make sense of the statement that we can love God in men, we can go further and try to see whether it makes sense also to speak of loving men in God. There is a difference of emphasis. In the first instance, the emphasis is on the discovery of God. In the second, the emphasis is on the enhancement of human love. It seems to me that such a manner of speaking is called for by the need to distinguish between two quite opposed ways of loving men, one selfish and the other unselfish. God is excluded from the first but appears in the second. The force of the preposition "in" confirms the impression that lovers sometimes have that their love is not wholly their own but resides within a love greater than what they know each other to be capable of. Admittedly, we are speaking of the human imagination. And we should not underestimate its function in the straining of the mind

[7] Jeremiah 22:15.

70

to understand the nature of human acts and intentions. If distinctions were not needed, we would not invent language to express them. Once again, it would be better if we left the names of God to the professional theologians. The best of them will always say in the end, as did St. Thomas Aquinas, "It's all straw." Would that they said it at the beginning.

8.

THE BEGINNING AND
THE END OF LOVE

A<small>N AFFAIR</small> has a beginning and an end in time, both observable. Two people meet, later part, and they can count the stages of their love along the way. Sometimes even after they part, or after one of them has died, they feel no diminishing of love and so discover that love has not ended after all. Less often do we question the beginning of love. So grounded in time and its moments, we are satisfied with measuring the before and the after of conscious love. It is only when we wonder how it could have happened to us that the word "beginning" takes on the meaning of cause. Who can tell how love comes about, what causes it? Who is not astonished that some people are loved by anyone? Yet rare is the person who is not loved by someone, if only his mother or father. " 'When you love you wish to do things for. You wish to sacrifice for. You wish to serve.' "[1] This is the end, the purpose of love, and it can persist beyond partings.

The end, the purpose, is also the beginning, the motive. And this too can be experienced. We do not notice it as much because, living always ahead of ourselves, we seldom take time out to ask how it all began. If we did, we would be stumped. How did it begin? Did we do something to make it begin? Did we deserve it? Did we ask for it? And the answer may well be "no." Where did this unselfish love come from? Surely not from the self that wants to be pampered, that wants to possess. Where then did it come from?

[1] Ernest Hemingway, *A Farewell to Arms* (New York: Scribner's, 1957), p. 75.

73

Where did our love for someone else come from, why should anyone have stopped his own concerns to care for us? Of course, these questions are not asked, at least very sincerely, by any who assume they are loadstones of love. They can be asked only by one who does not rate himself highly. Humility safeguards.

The classical description of the beginning of love comes from the first epistle of St. John: "Herein is love, not that we loved God, but that he loved us. . . . We love him, because he first loved us."[2] Obviously this does not describe want, desire. Men and women wander about the earth needing love and knowing it, but not finding it. They need love from any source, from man or from God. They need existential love, they need mystical love. Some are satisfied by one without the other, some only by both. I speak now only of what we suppose. For it may be that neither kind of love comes really separate from the other.

Let us think of someone who does not love. What will it take to get him started? It takes someone else's love for him. He needs to believe in love, just as he needs to believe in himself. And he may begin to love once he has seen a gratuitous act of love, either toward himself or toward someone else. He will love because he was loved first. And similarly he could not seek God unless he himself were not, so to speak, the matter of the sacrament, the spirit of which he was seeking. The sacrament points, but it also has power and the power is the motive for the seeking. Again, this has been said over and over because men have discovered in the end of the seeking the same power that they remembered as characteristic of the seeking itself. This is what Pascal meant when he said, "You would not seek me, if you had not found me."[3] Or, St. Bernard, " 'You would

[2] I St. John 4:10.

[3] *Pensées*, No. 554 (New York: Dutton, 1954).

74

not seek Him at all, O soul, nor love Him at all, if you had not been first sought and first loved. You have been anticipated by a twofold benediction, that of love and of seeking. The love is the cause of the seeking; the seeking is the fruit and clear proof of the love.' "[4]

If the end of the search is present in the beginning, the end of loving is also present in the beginning. There is a difference, however, between the nature of our seeking and loving, and God's finding and loving us. When we become aware of God's love, it is because we have become aware of grace, a gift unmerited. To say that God is not obliged to love us is not a way of saying that he may or may not, but rather that there is nothing about us that obliges anyone to love us. Once loved, we do have an obligation to render thanks and to return that love, for love that does not give is only one-way desire. And so we try to give as much as we have received. This is the nature of love, to attempt to keep up with grace. St. Catherine of Siena puts this very plainly:

> "I require that you should love Me with the same love with which I love you. This indeed you cannot do, because I loved you without being loved. All the love which you have for Me you owe to Me, so that it is not of grace that you love Me, but because I owe you My love. Therefore to Me, in person, you cannot repay the love which I require of you, and I have placed you in the midst of your fellows, that you may do to them that which you cannot do to Me, that is to say, that you may love your neighbor of free grace, without expecting any return from him, and what you do to him, I count as done to Me."[5]

This means that whenever one man loves another gratuitously, and not in response to his love, it is because he is, whether he realizes it or not, carrying out an obligation to God to do to others as He has done to us. Once again we

---

[4] *On Loving God*, p. 125.   [5] *The Soul Afire*, p. 273.

are empowered to do so because we believe in this kind of thing, we feel ourselves already part of that "territory of trust."[6] And just as we know well that we cannot match the freedom and therefore the intrinsic power of God's love for us, so we should not expect the human beings we love to match our initiative in response to us. They may do so only with others in their turn. Perhaps it is better for us if they do.

Greene's Sarah Miles said, " 'If I loved God, then I would believe in His love for me. It's not enough to need it. We have to love first, and I don't know how.' "[7] God showed her, by accepting her "offering" and reviving her lover. She did not know how, until she was shown. Nor did Bendrix know how until, having read her diary, he began to understand her and her sacrificed love. He had fled in self-hate and suspicion; he would continue to flee by hating a God who had robbed him of his love. But already his flight had become a pretense, as he committed himself to care for the husband he and Sarah had wronged.

> I fled Him, down the nights and down the days;
> I fled Him, down the arches of the years;
> I fled Him, down the labyrinthine ways
> Of my own mind.[8]

But, as Max Picard has written in *The Flight from God*, "Whithersoever they may flee, there is God. Wherever they find themselves, once more they flee away, for God is everywhere. Ever more desperately they flee; but God is already in every place, waiting for them to come. . . . Ever more desperately they fling themselves away, but they can only fling themselves so far, because they have torn themselves away from God. Only he who recoils from the

[6] Graham Greene, *The Heart of the Matter* (New York: Viking Press, 1962), p. 510.
[7] *The End of the Affair*, p. 112.
[8] Francis Thompson, *The Hound of Heaven*.

stability of God can fling himself so far."[9] And so the violence of flight from God seems to match the stability of God. It is the power of God transformed into fear instead of into desire. Sooner or later this fear, demoniacal as both Picard and Kierkegaard have told us, comes to the end of the finite, in the darkness of God. For some, surrender in darkness means death, as far as this soul can go; to others it means a new beginning: "Yet God's power is still manifested in man's tearing himself away from God. And only because God does not cease to go after those who have torn themselves away from him can they continue to flee on and on with such desperation. They are being hunted by God, and they move so swiftly only because he hunts them. Even this is God's love, that he, he and no other, wills to pursue the fleeing, so that he, the swiftest, may always be the nearest to those in flight."[10] Picard's " 'following love' "[11] is, as we can see, a gloss on Psalm 139. It is particularly relevant to an age like ours in which most men are, without knowing or caring, part of the flight. Whatever analogies may be drawn between Sarah Miles and Heloise, it is Bendrix' distance from Heloise that shows the distance mankind has sadly traveled since the twelfth century. Heloise did not have to learn to love; this was part of her obligation to God which, without approving of God's handling of her case, she knew how to deal with. Even Sarah had to learn from scratch, unless we are to believe that her baptism, unknown to her, had given her the sacramental power that enabled her to imitate God's sacrifice of Himself for mankind. However difficult their separation, both Heloise and Abelard found a vocation in a service with other women and with other men that

[9] *The Flight from God* (Chicago: Henry Regnery Co., 1951), p. 182.
[10] *Ibid.*
[11] Underhill, *Mysticism*, pp. 135–36.

was intended to be an exercise in divine charity. Sarah's vocation seems to have been to die, and Bendrix' to live in resentment, masking the rudiments of unselfish love. What we have seen in both affairs is a pattern of eternal love—existential—with an occasional hint or glimpse of the love sustaining it—mystical.

9.

THE IMPLICIT LOVE OF GOD

IF YOU have ever been in love, you will remember that
churning world in which all inhibitions disappeared and
you thought you were just then beginning to live. This
world of "being in love" is the model for Buber's I-Thou.
Only one who has offered himself unreservedly—rightly
or wrongly—to one other person can know what Buber
(and Sarah Miles) means by thinking of someone else
as "you." Parenthetically, it has always seemed to me un-
helpful to translate the German "du" as "Thou." This
archaism is laden with a formality, supported by Bible and
Prayer Book usage (also misunderstood, of course), that
only an old-fashioned Quaker would not feel. Perhaps
English speakers now do address God in the second person
plural, as a result. One way around the difficulty is to put
aside any attempt at literal translation and to talk first of
"thinking of" someone else as "you" before we talk of
"addressing" him as "you." For unfortunately too often
we use "you" with nearly the same lack of intimacy as is
implied in "hey, you." To think of someone else as "you"
implies that even his first name is an unnecessary barrier
to intimacy; to take the next step and write to someone as
"you," without using his name, again implies that this is
the only person whom we would address that way. And so
when we meet again, the ambivalent "you" is charged with
a special meaning.

The important thing, of course, is not the mode of
address but the unreserved quality of it. Do I hold something back still, and, conversely, am I ready to listen

79

unreservedly? Again, only those "in love" experience this freedom with any ease. For the rest of us, it is extremely difficult—and usually extremely imprudent—to try. What Buber had in mind involves a gift of the self that should not be identified with candor. Candor is a two-edged sword that one can brandish to show off as much as to assist. Genuinely personal concern is as likely to be shown by silence, by acts of kindness, as well as by assurances. The important thing is to withhold nothing of oneself that can be of service to others.

What is singular about Buber's point of view is his repeated insistence that in unreserved attentiveness to another person we meet God: "In each 'you' we meet the eternal 'You.' "[1] This statement is blunted somewhat by another: "Every particular 'you' is a glimpse through to the eternal 'You'; in other words, by means of every particular 'you' the primary world addresses the eternal 'You.' "[2] This is not the same as saying that when we address a human being, we address God at the same time. That sentence can mean two things: first, that in order to address God we must address man, and second, that when we address man we address God at the same time and in the same being, within man. In the first instance man addresses God by analogy, in the second because of identity. ("For unless you were in me, I could not exist.")

The question is whether man is felt to be a symbol of God (image) or a sacrament (both human image and something of divine power). Do we "touch" God (to use Greene's word) by means of touching men, or do we touch God when we touch men? The approach to God by way of symbol is the way of the vision and dream; the approach to God by immanence is the way of ecstasy. Each depends on a different kind of human experience, and there-

[1] *I and Thou*, p. 101.   [2] *Ibid.*, p. 75.

fore Buber, without remarking on this difference, is correct in suggesting both ways. What kind of experience makes a man think of God? Is it the same kind that impresses itself as a meeting with God? It may be, and the difference may be partly one of intensity (the source of the ecstasy, the transcendence) or of surprise and gratefulness (the sources of vision). A woman loves a man so much that both forget themselves entirely and feel only what is "between" them (Buber's preposition); they live, if only momentarily, in some space between them while they are "in" love. Or, a man is so astonished that someone loves him that he feels he must attribute this "grace" to a third who is beside them and whose divine existence he assumes for the occasion. "When he who abhors the name [God] and believes himself to be godless, gives his whole being to addressing the 'you' of his life, as a 'you' who cannot be limited by another, he is addressing God."[3] This is something more than going to the end of the finite and coming to the "unfathomable." Rather, Buber's encounters of man with man yield theological insights only because something positive is discovered that is totally new and not comprehensible in terms of previous experience.

Usually men think of God as something known rather than someone experienced. God can then be envisaged as a product of intellectual process. When this is tried, and fails, the reality of God seems implausible. Just so do we misapply the process of seeking-finding to God. Buber is emphatic about this: "There is no such thing as seeking God, for there is nothing in which He could not be found. How foolish and hopeless would be the man who turned aside from the course of his life in order to seek God. . . . His sense of 'you,' which cannot be satiated till he finds the

[3] *Ibid.*, p. 76.

endless 'You' had the 'You' present to it from the beginning; the presence had only to become wholly real to him in the reality of the hallowed life of the world."[4] At this point a medieval Christian, Lady Julian of Norwich, for example, would say, "God is nearer to us than our own soul: for He is the ground in whom our soul standeth." God as "the ground of our beseeching" or "the ground of our being" is the reality discovered in the initimacy of personal encounters that "makes all things new," "makes all things well."

And so for Buber there need be no conflict between existential and mystical, between the world and God: "I know nothing of a world and a life in the world that might separate a man from God. . . . Men do not find God if they stay in the world. They do not find Him if they leave the world. . . . Meeting with God does not come to man in order that he may concern himself with God, but in order that he may confirm that there is meaning in the world."[5] Does this mean that there is no validity to mysticism apart from love of the world? Is God to be met only in the world? If men do not find God either in the world or out of the world, where do they find God? This appears to be an absurd disjunction, a product of Buber's fondness for paradox. But wherever the encounter takes place, the main question is what kind of encounter it is: is it an intellectual encounter or is it, as the Christian mystics have said, a union? Is Buber, like Tillich, closer to Plotinus than to St. John of the Cross? Is it meaning or presence that man finds? Buber said both.

[4] *Ibid.*, p. 80.   [5] *Ibid.*, p. 95.

10.

THE BEAUTY OF THIS WORLD

SIMONE WEIL was never intentionally ambivalent or ambiguous. She took very seriously the biblical maxim "No man has seen God at any time" and began her essay on "Forms of the Implicit Love of God" by saying categorically (as usual) that "God is not present to the soul and has never yet been so."[1] Love of God is possible only as love of something else—religious ceremonies, the beauty of the world, and our neighbor. Explicit love is, strictly speaking, out of the question since God is never present; only implicit love can relate man to God at all. Existence must be thought of as a preparatory period, and love of God has to be a veiled love until in another life we see Him face to face. God does not love men directly either, but only through men. If He wishes to show his love for the afflicted, He waits until we consent to let His love work through us. And so it is really God who does the loving, we only consent to let Him love in our territory. If this sounds like a despairing separation of God from the world, it at least comes closer to the actual situation in which we find ourselves than the conventional piety that talks of God helping men in need directly. Such talk has made more cynics than converts. Men have always—from Job and the Psalmists to Albert Camus—observed that God is conspicuous by His absence when men are being persecuted, unless there are human protectors around.

One might well ask why Simone Weil thought she needed God at all as an explanation of human compassion.

---

[1] *Waiting for God*, p. 137.

She would answer by saying that "the true center is out-side the world"[2] and that the best in this world only points beyond the world. The best, or as she calls it, beauty, is the order of the world, and the "only finality here below": "It is because beauty has no end in view that it constitutes the only finality here below. . . . Only beauty is not the means to anything else. It alone is good in itself, but with-out our finding any particular good or advantage in it. It seems itself to be a promise and not a good.[3] And so beauty alone is to be loved. It may be "mutilated, distorted, soiled," but it is the "trap" set by God, the "labyrinth" into which man wanders, at the heart of which the Gorgon is a God waiting to devour man. This curious Jewish woman who rejected her own Jewishness, who went out of her way to look ugly, understood more about the economy of beauty than anyone since the writer of the Song of Songs. " 'Beauty is a fearful and a terrible thing,' " said Dmitri Karamazov. " 'It makes me mad that a man of great heart and high intelligence should begin with the idea of Madonna and end with the ideal of Sodom.' "[4] Yes, beauty can be a trap in more ways than one, and it is not necessarily God who waits in the labyrinth. And those who are born into this world beautiful have a special responsibility. Dostoevsky's portrait of Natasya Filippovna in *The Idiot* makes this unforgettably vivid. Her beauty was too much for her. "That dazzling beauty was quite unbearable . . . such beauty is power. . . . With such beauty one can turn the world up-side down."[5]

Romano Guardini in his essay on this novel says that "Natasya Filippovna is the being who by natural disposi-

[2] *Ibid.*, p. 160.

[3] *Ibid.*, pp. 165–66.

[4] *The Brothers Karamazov*, trans. David Magarshack (Baltimore: Penguin, 1958), p. 123.

[5] *The Idiot*, Part I, ch. 7, trans. David Magarshack (Baltimore: Penguin, 1955), pp. 108–9.

tion lives under the category of perfection. In her life all values seem to be strained to extremes. . . . Myshkin too is by nature ordained to perfection."[6] And Myshkin too is beautiful in an unearthly way. We may put these insights together briefly by saying that when we call the order of this world, or the whole presence of a person, beautiful it is really a vision of perfection that inspires us. Simone Weil adds to this the suggestion that "the beauty of the world is the co-operation of divine wisdom in creation."[7] And when she speaks, fancifully, of "Christ's tender smile for us coming through matter,"[8] we can see another point of difference between herself and Buber. For if Buber thought of man as a window to God, she, less optimistically, thought that there might be in men and matter some reflection of the Incarnation which men long for. "The longing to love the beauty of the world in a human being is essentially the longing for the Incarnation. It is mistaken if it thinks it is anything else. The Incarnation alone can satisfy it. It is therefore wrong to reproach the mystics, as has been done sometimes, because they use love's language. It is theirs by right. Others only borrow it."[9] Buber's world of I-You does not seem to need an Incarnation; there is no place in it for longing either. The opposition between his confidence and Simone Weil's pathos is very strong, whether because Buber had so much less sense of evil and malice than Dostoevsky, or whether he was complacent about the ease with which God can be found in human experience. Yet the Incarnation that Simone Weil longed for, something in her rejected, in love and in fear. She loved Christ and she feared baptism into the Body of Christ.

[6] "Dostoyevsky's Idiot: A Symbol for Christ," *Cross Currents*, Fall, 1956, p. 362.
[7] *Waiting for God*, p. 164.
[8] *Ibid.*, p. 165.
[9] *Ibid.*, p. 172.

" 'Be what you see, and receive what you are,' "[10] St. Augustine said. Be the Body of Christ. No one in modern times has understood what this means better than Simone Weil and Gerard Manley Hopkins. We are already His body.

I say móre: the just man justices;
Kéeps gráce: thát keeps all his goings graces;
Acts in God's eye what in God's eye he is—
Chríst—for Christ plays in ten thousand places,
Lovely in limbs, and lovely in eyes not his
To the Father through the features of men's faces.[11]

We are particularly His Body when we consent to God's love for the afflicted being administered by Him through us. The world also is His Body—has not all creation been redeemed?

The world is charged with the grandeur of God.[12]

There lives the dearest freshness deep down in things.[13]

Nothing is so beautiful as spring.[14]

Look at the stars! Look, look up at the skies![15]

Brute beauty and valour and act, oh, air, pride, plume here
    Buckle![16]

Summer ends now; now, barbarous in beauty, the stooks arise.[17]

As we drove home the stars came out thick; I leant back to look at them and my heart opening more than usual praised our Lord to and in whom all that beauty comes home.[18]

---

[10] Sermon 272, *An Augustine Synthesis*.
[11] Hopkins, poem 34.
[12] Hopkins, "God's Grandeur."
[13] *Ibid*.
[14] Hopkins, "Spring."
[15] Hopkins, "The Starlight Night."
[16] Hopkins, "The Windhover."
[17] Hopkins, "Hurrahing in Harvest."
[18] Hopkins, *Journals and Papers*, Aug. 17, 1874, ed. Humphrey House (London: Oxford University Press, 1959).

Yet Simone Weil was certain that the true center is outside the world. Does this mean that she instinctively thought of Christ as having been a visitor who came, left footprints, and went off again, leaving us to our devices, our consent, and our rejection? It looks like that. But the poignancy of her life and reflections pales beside the darkness of Hopkins' "terrible sonnets."[19] It is as if an acceptance of the Incarnation amid this beautiful dark world entails profoundest suffering. "My taste was me."[20] Only the redeemed man can afford the luxury of the dark night of the soul.

Between Buber and Weil on the one hand, and Hopkins on the other, between prophecy and longing on the one hand, and redemption on the other, is common beauty, the carnal beauty of this world. It is there to serve us.

> Carnal love in all its forms . . . has the beauty of the world as its object. The love we feel for the splendor of the heavens, the plains, the sea, and the mountains, for the silence of nature which is borne in upon us by thousands of tiny sounds, for the breath of the winds or the warmth of the sun, this love of which every human being has at least an inkling, is an incomplete, painful love because it is felt for things incapable of responding. . . . Men want to turn this same love toward a being who is like themselves and capable of answering to their love, of saying yes, of surrendering. When the feeling for beauty happens to be associated with the sight of some human being, the transference of love is made possible, at any rate in an illusory matter. But it is all the beauty of the world, it is universal beauty for which we yearn.[21]

So speaks a woman who felt that love of another person is illusory, and that when we see beauty in another it is God we are looking for implicitly. She may be right. There is much in our experience that would suggest this, everything except for some joy which seems sufficient in itself,

---

[19] Poems 41–46.   [20] Hopkins, poem 44.
[21] Weil, *Waiting for God*, p. 171.

an unquenchable belief in the beauty of this world, no matter how illusory our experience of it. "Beauty is eternity here below,"[22] and for some that is enough. Buber should have said this.

Here below, "the country of here below," "the city of the world,"[23] our place of exile, we have beauty alone to guide us, in religious ceremonies and in our love for our neighbor. "We feel ourselves to be outsiders, uprooted, in exile here below. We are like Ulysses who had been carried away during his sleep by sailors and woke in a strange land, longing for Ithaca with a longing that rent his soul. Suddenly Athena opened his eyes and he saw that he was in Ithaca. In the same way every man who longs indefatigably for his country . . . will one day suddenly find that he is there."[24] More conscious of her exiled nature than Buber, Simone Weil guarded with tragic determination the pass between the two cities, and between the existential and the mystical. And yet her encouragement of "filial piety" toward the country here below was similar to that enjoined by Hopkins in his poem "To what serves Mortal Beauty":

> What do then? how meet beauty? | Merely meet it; own,
> Home at heart, heaven's sweet gift; | then leave, leave that
>   alone.
> Yea, wish that though, wish all, | God's better beauty, grace.

Accept beauty, accept the world, accept the neighbor, accept all the gifts and leave categories and judgments to God.

[22] *Ibid.*, p. 172.   [23] *Ibid.*, p. 175.   [24] *Ibid.*, p. 178.

III

11.

THE IMAGERY OF LOVE

ELIZABETH BARRETT wrote many letters of love to Robert Browning, and we know that in them she was expressing her love for him, and not for God. The Portuguese Nun wrote love letters to a French count and no one has ever mistaken her for a mystic either. When St. Maria Maddalena de' Pazzi and St. Mechthild of Magdeburg yearned for God and used the same words that a woman uses for her love of a man, we do not doubt that they loved God rather than man. Arthur Symons said of St. John of the Cross, "This monk can give lessons to lovers!" And we do not suppose he could because he had had an affair with a woman before he became a monk; we do not wonder whether he had a woman in mind when he wrote *The Spiritual Canticle*. With these, and with many more, we know where we are. We know whether their love was either existential or mystical.

But when we turn to the Bible and read the Song of Songs, we are in trouble. God is not mentioned at all. And yet we wonder how this song could remain in the Bible if it is not religious in some way. If we are reading the King James Version, help is given by the headings at the top of each column. "The church's love unto Christ," "The love of Christ and his church," "The graces of the church," "A description of Christ by his graces," "The church's graces, and love to Christ." They are a little repetitious, but then the text does not mention Christ, his graces, or the church, and it is unfair to accuse the translators of not being more imaginative. It is sad, however, to

91

discover that these assurances have gone unrewarded in recent years: the Song of Songs is no longer read in Anglican churches (although it is still read as part of the Jewish Passover liturgy).

The history of interpretation of the Song of Songs is fascinating and amusing. Written several centuries before Christ (so obviously it was not intended to be about him or his church), it was regarded as part of holy writ by pious Jews even before the question was settled once and for all by Rabbi Akiba at the Council of Jamnia in 100 A.D. when he said, "All the Hagiographa are holy, but the *Canticle* is most holy." It is also reported that Rabbi Akiba reminded those who had been singing it in cabarets: "Anyone who for the sake of entertainment sings the Song as though it were a profane song, will have no share in the World to come." Most Jewish commentators followed his lead and have insisted that the poem describes God's love for Israel. And since Christians assumed that the Church was the New Israel, the way was prepared for them to incorporate it in their canon too. Origen, St. Ambrose, St. Gregory the Great, and St. Jerome put the weight of their authority behind the allegorical reading of it. Not that they were unaware of difficulties facing the unwary or the innocent. St. Jerome, author of the Vulgate translation, even took time out to counsel a friend for the sake of her daughter, "Let her never look upon her own nakedness. She should not read *The Song of Songs* until she has read *Chronicles* and *Kings*, for otherwise she might not observe that the book refers only to spiritual love." We do not know why he preferred Chronicles and Kings over the rest of the canon, but I feel confident that this would be very effective advice if followed today.

Long before the twelfth century the allegorical interpretation was established. It could be—and was—applied to anything. And yet even then St. Bernard of Clairvaux thought it necessary to caution the hearers of his eighty-six sermons on the Canticle: " 'Take heed that you bring chaste ears to this discourse of love; and when you think of these two lovers, remember always that not a man and a woman are to be thought of, but the Word of God and a Soul. And if I shall speak of Christ and the Church, the sense is the same, except that under the name of the Church is specified not one soul only, but the united souls of many, or rather their unanimity.' "[1] Today all the authority of St. Bernard and St. Jerome is not sufficient to persuade most readers to read the song allegorically. As C. S. Lewis and others have pointed out, allegory is, to say the least, a lost art of reading.

But it was not always thus, and, as Evelyn Underhill has remarked, the Song of Songs provided the imagery for many of the most original mystical writings in the Christian tradition.

> It has been said that the constant use of such imagery by Christian mystics of the mediaeval period is traceable to the popularity of the *Song of Songs*, regarded as an allegory of the spiritual life. I think that the truth lies rather in the opposite statement: namely, that the mystic loved the *Song of Songs* because he there saw reflected, as in a mirror, the most secret experiences of his soul. . . . The great saints who adopted and elaborated this symbolism, applying it to their pure and ardent passion for the Absolute, were destitute of the prurient imagination which their modern commentators too often possess.[2]

She is probably right, but that does not settle the question about the meaning of the Song of Songs. Both Christians and Jews found this poem in their respective canons; they had to do something with it. How it got there and what it

---

[1] Sermon 61 in Dom Cuthbert Butler, *Western Mysticism* (London: Arrow Books Ltd., 1960), p. 157.

[2] Underhill, *Mysticism*, p. 137.

meant in the first place is another and, to us, more interesting problem. Even today this poem challenges the pious, especially Catholic commentators. Typical of them is the following statement: "The most important problem in *Canticle* is its meaning and interpretation. Apparently *Canticle* is an erotic poem with or without a higher aim of describing love in its purest form or of extolling the excellence of monogamy or conjugal fidelity. This is the view prevailing among non-Catholic interpreters, and we have no right to introduce any other sense unless we have solid reasons, and these reasons must be sought for not in the book itself, but in other biblical books."[3] Surely one could not ask for a more candid approach. Yet how strange to modern ears is the suggestion that a text should be interpreted by looking for its meaning outside itself. Perhaps this is a last desperate attempt to do the impossible. But he is right in saying that non-Catholics are unanimous in looking on it as an erotic poem, although they are not unanimous as to whether it has any relevance to religion. Some would say that it has none, unless it is deliberately allegorized; others see that it is religious precisely because it is erotic (although they would not necessarily use this adjective).

Only recently has there been the beginning of a new way of looking at the Song.

> The *Song of Songs* is an authentic, that is, worldly love lyric; precisely for this reason, not in spite of it, it is a genuinely spiritual song for the love of God for man. The person loved only by God is locked against the whole world and locks himself up. This is the element in all mysticism which not only appears unwholesome to every natural feeling, but is in fact, objectively speaking, calamitous.[4]

[3] P. P. Saydon, *A Catholic Commentary on Holy Scripture* (New York: Nelson, 1953), p. 383.

[4] Franz Rosenzweig in *The Worlds of Existentialism*, ed. Maurice Friedman (New York: Random House, 1964), p. 328.

> Even the Bible can find room for the *Song of Songs*, and one could hardly have a more passionate and sensual love than is there portrayed. It is a good thing that that book is included in the Bible as a protest against those who believe that Christianity stands for the restraint of passion. . . . I must say, I prefer to read it as an ordinary love poem, which is probably the best Christological exposition too.[5]

Rosenzweig's suggestion is similar to Sarah Miles's " Was it really You I loved all the time,' " and Buber's "In each 'you' we address the eternal 'You.' " And it is just as ambiguous. Is there an identity of loving, or is human love being used by divine love? Bonhoeffer's guess that the poem can be expounded Christologically was never developed. We have, however, from Professor Daniel Lys a thoroughly argued exposition of this view: "The *Canticle* has a place in the canon because it says that human love is the very condition of the life of man. There is only one love, the second commandment is similar to the first. The love of man for God is manifested and realized in the love of man for his neighbor, and above all for the spouse who is the closest of his neighbors. Sexual love has in some way its end in itself. The divine love is the model for human love. The religious sense of the *Canticle* is in its literal sense."[6]

The alternative interpretations can be reduced to the following few: literal or figurative, and if figurative, then symbolizing history or the life of the spirit. Scholars will continue to debate the nature and source of fragments of the poem and wonder whether they are held together by any recognizable form. Was the poem written at one time by one person, an original work of art? Or is it a collection, an anthology, perhaps containing remnants of nuptial

[5] Bonhoeffer, *Letters and Papers from Prison*, p. 100.
[6] "Le plus beau chant de la création," *Etudes Théologiques Religieuses*, 1958. no. 4.

rites, songs, processions? Is it a series of songs, or a drama with voices? How many voices are there? And can a chorus be heard? These questions have encouraged scholars to think that the poem, written or put together with no explicit religious intent, had a religious interpretation imposed on it. A figurative interpretation could be used for the sake of reminding patriotic Jews of their own history, and religious Jews of the spiritual dimensions of that history. The latter could be called a mystical interpretation, using the word in the medieval sense. And according to such an interpretation, one could exclude the erotic sense once the spiritual sense was firmly in mind, or one could imagine eroticism itself building up to such a peak that it would explode—almost as a Dostoevskian epileptic vision —into spiritual ecstasy. The latter is a pagan approach to religion not unknown in our own time. But normally the disposition to choose a figurative interpretation goes hand in hand with a disposition to find sex embarrassing, or a genuine inability to see any meaning in sex as an end in itself. The puritanical, neurotic, view of sex (so similar to the Manicheism that corrupted St. Augustine and his successors in the Middle Ages) has been extraordinarily hard to exorcize.

I can summarize in another way. Some have thought that the Canticle was nothing more than a series of love poems, later given religious interpretations. Others have actually claimed that it was originally intended to be religious. Some have compromised and claimed that since both existential and mystical loves are real, it is right to hear both in the poem: love is one, and both existential and mystical loves follow a similar phenomenological pattern (non-transitive love). And, finally, others are convinced that the poem is religious precisely because it is secular.

Those holding the first, the literal, view say—and it is hard to refute—that there is no internal evidence for a mystical interpretation. And many readers today react with contempt against any who pretend to see in the poem what is not there, suspecting them of discarding that which they fear. Those who, like St. Bernard, really believe that it was written with a spiritual meaning in mind would not, in all probability, be upset if they were once and for all proved wrong. They could say, "No matter, it is still the best way man has to describe the mutual love of God and man." And for anyone who is used to shuttling back and forth between bed and Church, the erotic and the religious, it is not impossible to read a common pattern of a double life, longing for meaning. But the attitude most peculiar to our own time is the fourth, which holds that the real test of man's love for God is his love for other men, and for women—that love is always incarnate spirit.

It is usually safe to "take what the author said for what he meant to say,"[7] yet we have to agree with St. Bernard when he says that God has to use our terms to declare his wisdom.

> "Let us in the exposition of this sacred and mystical discourse proceed carefully, with simplicity of purpose, and follow the example of the Scripture itself, which declares the hidden wisdom in our human words, indeed, but in a mystery; and which in order to make God known to our powers of apprehension makes use of figurative language and imparts to human minds those precious truths, the unknown and invisible things of God, by means of similitudes drawn from things apparent to the senses, and, so to speak, proffers the draught of truth in cups formed of a material of little value."[8]

Of course, the final phrase, "material of little value," exposes St. Bernard's prejudices and rather detracts from the general truth of his remarks. These, however, are not

[7] *Ibid.*   [8] Sermon 74 in *Western Mysticism*, p. 120.

really applicable to the Song of Songs, for one thing is clear and consistent about the figurative language of the Bible—it is always plainly indicated. Whether the symbolism is an extended metaphor, like Hosea's likening of his unfortunate marriage to Gomer the prostitute to the whoring of Israel after false gods, with Hosea's pardon being compared to God's promised loving redemption of straying Israel, or, more simply, as in line metaphors such as "Just as the hart desires the waterbrooks, so longs my soul after you O God,"[9] it is always perfectly plain what is going on.

Similarly today it is perfectly plain to most readers that a girl is longing for a man and expresses herself in physical symbolism suitable to the circumstances. Is that not good enough? Biblical authors—and Jesus—are not hesitant about following up parables and allegories with explanations. Besides, since the Bible is replete with many descriptions of man's love for God and God's love for man, why should there not be room for at least one account of a woman's love for a man? Perhaps the answer is not so much that God's love for a man is more important, as that human love is not really important at all. In other words, the existential is and ought to be opposed to the mystical, as the inferior to the superior. Sex is an inferior kind of love, and if it cannot be avoided, it can be made use of. Its energies can be sublimated, and its language can be employed for a better kind of experience.

It is hardly possible to say this today without feeling a reverse kind of blasphemy, the indecency of putting into words a point of view generally felt to be absurd. Yet not so long ago it would have been the man who suggested that the Canticle is erotic who would have been called blasphemous. Theodore of Mopsuestia (fifth century) and

[9] Psalm 42.

Sebastien Castellio (sixteenth century) in their times were rather like the child who saw the emperor minus his clothes, except that they did not convince their fellow townsmen. They did not fare well, holding as they did that the Song of Songs meant exactly what it said. Perhaps it is presumptuous, in any case, to assume too glibly that this extraordinarily rich text of 117 verses will yield its meaning to the quick and vulgar reading of our century if it was worth 86 sermons of St. Bernard (and more, had he lived).

It is a maze and a mine of treasure to be sorted out with delight, unending critical delight. Clearly composed of a series of lyrics, some sung by a girl, some by a man, and interleaved with choral passages, it is distinguished by its Palestinian universe of allusions. In addition to the sixteen places named, the references to living creatures, jewels, artifacts, topics in landscape, food, drink, spices, and flowers provide the fullest bank from which to draw the lush metaphors for which the Canticle is justly famous. Surpassing all other poems in sensuous allusion, its main tone is nevertheless so direct as to be inescapably moving. "I" and "You" alternate in a rhythm of desire and aching anxiety, from the opening and closing lines to the nightmare of loss in chapter 5. The style passes with swift economy from the hortatory to the self-descriptive, to dialogue, to the choral, a succession of encomiums, each more intense than the one before it, visions, dreams, triumphal processional and pastoral, narrative and creed; and all rendered in a lyrical mode. The compactness alone sets it apart from other writings and lulls the reader into supposing a dramatic unity which may not be there at all.

Next to the figurative interpreter's bland assumption that the "bride" is "the soul thirsting for God," and the bridegroom is "the Word of God," is the equally questionable assumption that the girl's voice is the voice of a bride, and that there can be heard in the eight chapters a more or less clear sequence of betrothal, nuptial ceremony, ecstatic union, and the early fruits of marriage. We can find almost anything if we look hard enough: the question is can we hear all this without being told? I myself cannot dispose of the last verse ("Make haste, my beloved, and be like a gazelle or a young stag upon the mountains of spices"), so similar in its hortatory tone to the opening line ("O that you would kiss me with the kisses of your mouth!") just by saying it is obscure or a late addition. On the contrary, it seems very clear to me that the girl is no further along in her actual love affair—if she had one—at the end than at the beginning. But I have never heard anyone else say this. On the contrary, the usual interpretation divides the poem into a number of cantos, sung more or less alternately in duet, in which the progress of the wooing is recorded, from the initial desire to the final retrospective references to the girl's "little sister." As to this, it would seem to me just as right to think that she is speaking of herself, and not of a sister. And beyond that, I cannot find any passage which can be the basis for assuming a sexual union has occurred. The tenses are future: "I will climb the palm tree. . . . I will give you my love. . . . I would lead you. . . . I would give you. . . . O that his left hand were under my head." On the contrary, the more I have pored over the latter part of the poem, the more disposed I am to hear the anguished tones of a human being so much in love with someone else that he (or she) imagines the person and the course of love and is no nearer fulfillment at the end than at the beginning. On the whole, this interpretation seems to me more in keeping with the over-all tone of exquisite longing that is as strong in chapters 7 and 8 as in chapters 1 and 2.

100

"The Song of Songs, which is Solomon's" is a way of saying, "the best song of all," "the perfect song," of all creation. All creation is in the song, in the carefully accumulated allusions to the entire Palestinian scene, approached through all five senses. Is it any wonder that the dominant note is the recurrent praise of beauty, perfect, undefiled? "Behold, you are beautiful, my love." This lyric line is completed by the seven songs of adoration, each composed of a series of similes and metaphors, which have so delighted and embarrassed men, women, and children for over two thousand years.

There is nothing ambiguous about the way the poem begins, with a pleading for kisses and an exalting of the desired love ("your love is better than wine"). To call it erotic may be an unjustifiable prejudging of the nature of the love described. In the Septuagint version (the third-century B.C. Greek translation of the Old Testament) the words for love are *agape* and *eros*. The Hebrew also uses two words: *chashek*, which denotes physical desire, and *achavah*, which denotes love on all levels but more particularly love on a higher level.[10] St. Jerome used both *amor* and *caritas*. For once in the long history of the interpretation of this poem, it might be good to ask, as Professor Lys has asked, whether human love does not have its end in itself, and, therefore, whether all human love, sexual love and nuptial love, does not have sufficient importance to be incorporated in a theory of the totality of human experience. Once men stop depreciating themselves, they will be ready to value properly the significance of some of the passions they have tried to repress.

These 117 lines ring all the changes on the yearning of one heart for another, from desire to daydream to nightmare, with one following the other in broken order until

[10] For this I am indebted to Joel Glasser, one of my students at Johns Hopkins.

101

the spirit of the lover is cauterized and can cry only in the controlled fragments of desire that make up the final chapter. "Draw me . . . tell me," of chapter 1, lightly supported by the tender praises of verses 15 and 16, are only the prelude to the poignancy of the first part of chapter 2:

> With great delight I sat in his shadow,
>   and his fruit was sweet to my taste.
> He brought me to the banqueting house,
>   and his banner over me was love.
> Sustain me with raisins,
>   refresh me with apples;
>   for I am sick with love.

The sentiment and the language were written for St. Teresa of Ávila and St. John of the Cross to appropriate. More than two thousand years have not affected the transformation of desire into a throbbing sickness from love. The past tense in "I sat . . . he brought" may suggest a wish-dream rather than a recollection. Once this takes hold, the text poses no difficult problems. The rest of the chapter then reads as a daydream:

> The voice of my beloved!
>   Behold, he comes,
> . . . .
> Behold, there he stands
>   behind our wall,
> . . . .
> My beloved speaks and says to me:
>   Arise, my love, my fair one,
>   and come away.

Throughout the poem the lilting parallelism of the Hebrew verse, to which we are accustomed from the antiphonal reading of psalms, provides whatever ground swell of unity is needed to hold together the rise and fall of longing. There are moments when this longing strains upward almost unbearably, moments which are repeated in the same words in another place. Such are verses 6 and 7 in this chapter:

> O that his left hand were under my head,
>   and that his right hand embraced me!
> I adjure you, O daughters of Jerusalem,
>   by the gazelles or the hinds of the field,
> that you stir not up nor awaken love
>   until it please.

The pleading in the "O that" is transformed through a daydream and comes out at the other end in the simple affirmation of love's exclusiveness. "My beloved is mine and I am his," or as the Prayer Book says, "forsaking all others, keep thee only unto her," or in the words of the Irish charm: "I set a charm for love, a charm of love and desire: a charm of God that none can break.—You for me, and I for thee and for no other: your face to mine, and your head turned away from all."

The third chapter opens with a real dream of night. The yearning of the daytime, being unfulfilled, goes underground. In its matter-of-fact economy it could not be surpassed; it should remind most of us of a common enough dream sequence.

> Upon my bed by night
>   I sought him whom my soul loves;
> I sought him but found him not;
>   I called him, but he gave no answer.
> I will rise now and go about the city,
>   in the streets and in the squares;
> I will seek him whom my soul loves.
>   I sought him, but found him not.
> The watchmen found me,
>   as they went about the city.
> "Have you seen him whom my soul loves?"
> Scarcely had I passed them,
>   when I found him whom my soul loves.
> I held him, and would not let him go.

The realism of the dream, this dream and all dreams, comes from its mixture of wish and fate. The longing, the seeking, has not been killed by the absence—or even the indifference—of the loved one. "I sought him, but found him not" is the fate behind the wish. And the wish itself exceeds the possible, as in the last two lines: "When I found him . . . I held him." The dream lingers on when the soul awakens and, as in many such awakenings, a fervent appeal is made to put one's trust in the real person just imagined. In chapter 3 this appeal is followed—I might say tempted—by the hubris of the stately royal processional (a passage which has its peer only in Shakespeare's description of the meeting of Antony and Cleopatra upon the river of Cydnus).

Encouraged by the spontaneous dream the lover indulges herself by fancying the praises and adoration of the one she loves. Beginning with the words she would love most to hear (she who is "dark," "swarthy"), "Behold, you are beautiful," and singling out each of her own features for special praise, she likens herself to "a garden locked" but waiting to be opened by her imagined lover. The more she desires him, the more she fancies him desiring her—"You have ravished my heart, my sister, my bride." Her wishing ascends to the dramatic invocation, "Awake, O north wind. . . . Let my beloved come to his garden and eat its choicest fruits," and in her fantasy she imagines him replying, " I come to my garden. . . . I gather . . . I eat . . . I drink." Drugged into the tranquillity of her ecstatic revery, her own voice seals the flight with the choral line, "Eat, O friends, and drink: drink deeply, O lovers."

This euphoria is immediately followed, and shattered, by a second night dream. "I slept, but my heart was awake." While she sleeps she goes on hoping that her loved one will really come and beg to be taken in. At this point her deepest sense of reality intervenes, and, in a series of

104

frustrations each more bitter than the other, depresses the heart.

> I had put off my garment,
>> how could I put it on?
> I had bathed my feet,
>> how could I soil them?
> . . . .
> I arose to open to my beloved
>> and my hands dripped with myrrh,
> my fingers with liquid myrrh,
>> upon the handles of the bolt.
> I opened to my beloved,
>> but my beloved had turned and gone.
> My soul failed me when he spoke.
> I sought him, but found him not;
>> I called him, but he gave no answer.

Who in a dream has not tried to take a step and not been able to move a foot, reached out a hand and not been able to touch, called and been ignored? The heart knows what daydreaming would deny. And in the night the heart speaks, to correct the soul when it has buried desire, to correct again when its desires have outrun reality.

Once before, in a dream, she had imagined herself alone in the street searching for her lover (like Swann looking for Odette) yet finding only the watchmen (and, like Swann, meeting her lover unexpectedly when she had given up). Again she wanders the city streets at night, and again the watchmen find her. But this time they beat her and humiliate her. In her despair she invokes the good offices of her friends, "I adjure you, O daughters of Jerusalem," but not with the confidence of chapter 2, verse 7, "that you stir not up nor awaken love until it please," but in humbled pathos, "if you find my beloved, tell him I am sick with love."

The soul in love cannot be suppressed, by disappointment or by truth. Each time felled, love springs up more strongly than before. The cynical, "what is your beloved more than another beloved" is not only followed up with panegyrics of the lover, but with two paeans setting forth her own loveliness. The whole world in all its beauty lies reflected in her beauty. All creation participates by analogy in the imagined perfection of a self so beautiful it cannot help being loved. To compare the adoration of her body in chapter 4 with the even more famous one in chapter 7 is to remark at once that whereas the description there began more innocently with eyes and hair before moving down to the breasts, here the praises travel upward from feet and thighs, to head and locks. And as the eye approaches her:

> You are stately as a palm tree,
>   and your breasts are like its clusters.
> I say I will climb the palm tree
>   and lay hold of its branches.

She then finishes her ecstatic revery by breathing acceptance, and in words which she has used once before to conclude a daydream:

> I am my beloved's,
>   and his desire is for me.

If this is sexual imagery, and if she dreams of a union that is still denied her, she has learned by now how to live with her own dreams. She does not need to be shocked into reality by a nightmare; on the contrary, she knows how to keep her balance by shifting to less fevered fancies, as one finds at the beginning of chapter 8.

> O that you were like a brother to me . . .
> . . . .
> If I met you outside, I would kiss you,
>   and none would despise me.
> I would lead you and bring you
>   into the house of my mother.

106

Then we hear snatches of desires that, when we heard them
before, were parts of more intense, heavier yearning.

> O that his left hand were under my head,
>> and that his right hand embraced me!
> I adjure you, O daughters of Jerusalem,
>> that you stir not up nor awaken love until it please.

The rest of the poem consists of fragmentary bursts of
reminiscence, faith, self-pity, self-offering.

One interpretation can be as fanciful as another. The
poem defies definitive analysis. Perhaps it does not matter
in the end whether we see a dramatic progression or a
dream sequence, something accomplished or something
fancied. Running through the waves of longing is, as
Bonhoeffer has said, "a kind of *cantus firmus*, to which the
other melodies of life provide the counterpoint." That
cantus firmus can be heard all by itself in verses 6 and 7 of
chapter 8.

> Set me as a seal upon your heart,
>> as a seal upon your arm;
> For love is strong as death,
>> jealously cruel as the grave.
> Its flashes are flashes of fire,
>> a most vehement flame.
> Many waters cannot quench love,
>> neither can floods drown it.
> If a man offered for love all the wealth of his house,
>> it would be utterly scorned.

Like the ode to love in Sophocles' *Antigone*, these verses
affirm, almost in credal accents, the unconquerable power
of love. The lover would like to be bound, as a reminder,
to the heart and hand ("Give me your heart, give me your
hand") of the one she loves, as a phylactery is bound to
the head and arm of the orthodox Jew. Inside the phylactery
is the declaration of faith: "Hear, O Israel: The Lord our

God is one Lord; and you shall love the Lord your God with all your heart, and with all your soul, and with all your might."[11] Believe in me, she says: I am to be your faith, as near as your heart, as close as your hand. Worship me.

What pious Jew, reading these verses, would not think of the *tephillin* and notice the placing of the first seal on the heart instead of the head? This but reinforces the earlier affirmations of belonging: "My beloved is mine, and I am his." And, by implication, they can never be parted, in spite of all the separations of longing and despair, of failed love. "My soul failed me," yet, "Many waters cannot quench love." These two lines contain the extremes of reality and dream that constitute a course of longing that runs freely through vision and depression to its validation of hope.

But the pious Jew—like the pious Christian—may look on this echo of pious practice as proof of the religious meaning of the Song of Songs. He should, however, contain his jubilation, unless he is willing to consider the nature of that religion with unprejudiced eyes. The Jew knows something of God's covenant with Israel; the Christian knows something of "the spiritual marriage and unity betwixt Christ and His Church."[12] They do not believe their own earthly marriages bring about their salvation, any more than they bring about the covenanted union of God and Israel. But believing in the divine marriage, they feel liberated for their human marriages, and for the same close, mystical union one with another. It is not that we learn here of the love of God for man, modeled on human love, but that having known God's love for man, we now know more about human love. And knowing more, we aim at more. St. Paul said, "Husbands, love your wives

[11] Deuteronomy 6:4–5.
[12] "Marriage Service," *The Book of Common Prayer.*

108

as Christ loved the Church."[13] Married love should be that close, that indissoluble, that sacrificial, that mutual. One thing more—if married love, existential love, is to succeed, it can have no divided loyalties, any more than the love of man for God or God for man. God alone must be adored, not false gods, not idols. And God will not create man and then turn away and go about some other business; we are His business. Likewise, no other love must be allowed to interject itself between man and man, not even man's love for God. For to do this would be, in effect, to misconceive the nature of God.

If man is to love God with all his heart and soul, he must do so by loving his neighbor as himself. "Inasmuch as ye have done it unto one of the least of these my brethren, ye have done it unto me." Or, as Lys says, "We can love Him, true God, only in loving him, true man, and so we can love God with our whole heart only in loving our neighbor gratuitously and without after-thought."[14] This is the significance of the love of man for Jesus Christ, true man and true God, the meaning of "mediator." For if by loving Jesus Christ, true man, because he is true God, we may yet learn the harder lesson of loving true man, and true woman also, because they are human and are made in God's image. The man who thinks he loves God but is indifferent to his neighbor, the woman who spends her life in religious observance and is contemptuous of carnal love, misconceives the nature of loving God. For what does it mean for a man to love God, but to love what is at hand, man, woman, child, and all the rest of creation? Is God something quite apart from this, in the way a thought is abstracted from experience? Mystical love set apart from existential love will be a dreadful chimera, deluding man

[13] Ephesians 5:25.
[14] "Le plus beau chant de la création," p. 115.

into missing out on his actual destiny. Existential love of the kind the writer of the Song of Songs dreamed about is the very condition of mystical love, inspired by a holy spirit which demands a perfect imitation.

In real life both Christians and Jews have preferred the security of figurative readings of this song, just as both Catholic and Protestant Christians have accepted the compartmentalization of love into existential and mystical. Jewish tradition is not puritanical. In fact, the orthodox code of ethics (*shulchan orach*) recommends to husbands and especially to scholars that they begin the sabbath observance on Friday night by having intercourse with their wives.[15] For them this "good thing" is a religious act. It is not surprising, therefore, that until very recently certain strains of orthodox Judaism alone held that the religious sense of the Song is to be found in the literal sense.

[15] See note 10.

110

12.

THE SEVEN STAGES OF LOVE

S T. John of the Cross is best known for his "negative
way," and more especially for "the dark night of the
soul." His reputation arises more from his four theological
commentaries on his poems than from the poems themselves. No wonder that he has been called "the poet of the
minus sign."[1] We would do well to remember that although
he wrote the commentaries for the edification of nuns and
monks, he wrote the poems for himself. In the prologue
to the commentary on *The Spiritual Canticle* he advises the
Reverend Mother who had commissioned the work that
"it would be foolish to think that expressions of love
arising from mystical understanding, like these stanzas,
are fully explainable. The spirit of the Lord, who abides in
us and aids our weakness, pleads for us with unspeakable
groanings in order to manifest what we can neither fully
understand nor comprehend. . . . I cannot explain ade-
quately, nor is it my intention to do so." Unfortunately,
no one else has tried very hard either. The religious scribes
are content to reprint the commentaries in new translations,
while the literati have gone out of their way to set poetry
into English that fails to show either the literal meaning or
the poetic economy of the Spanish. St. John's poems have
now become about as well known to readers of poetry as
the Song of Songs and as little examined. Perhaps it is St.
John's fault. He is known to have been a mystic, and he
wrote conventional ascetical commentaries—which means

[1] Gerald Brenan, "Studies in Genius: St. John of the Cross," *Horizon*, May
and June, 1947.

111

that his poetry represents mystical experiences that are foreign to most twentieth-century people. It is interesting, therefore, that the poems should not only be read now, but that they should give real pleasure.

There is no question that St. John was a mystic, and there is not the slightest reason to think he had ever had a love affair. The four commentaries not only exhibit his familiarity with the Western mystical tradition and the systematic theology of St. Thomas Aquinas, they describe in some detail St. John's own contemplative methods. These would probably be of little or no interest to anyone but a religious these days were it not for their relationship to three of his poems. And even here especially in reading *The Dark Night of the Soul*, some acquaintance with his life in and escape from the monastic prison in Toledo can be enlightening. The two commentaries on this poem, *The Ascent of Mt. Carmel* and *The Dark Night of the Soul*, treat exhaustively the major difficulties encountered by contemplatives in their life of prayer, but, apart from the fact that they only cover about two stanzas, they by no means exhaust the meaning of the poem to one who is not a contemplative. This poem, and the others, have lives of their own because they are great poems, produced by a mind more subtle than its pedestrian analyses of obstacles to prayer. The originality of St. John's poetic vision has yet to be precisely located and acknowledged.

Indeed, if we should take the poem *The Dark Night of the Soul* by itself as a test, it is apparent not only that the two commentaries do not exhaust even the first two stanzas, but that they are not even talking about them. If St. John did not tell us, how could we know that this poem in any way described the same dark night of the soul that he outlines in such clarity of detail in the commentary of that name? Where in the poem is there any sense of the night as "horrible and awful"?[2] Where is the impression conveyed of a "cruel spiritual death" or of "the clear perception, as it thinks, that God has abandoned it," or "that all creatures have forsaken it"?[3] It is not there. It seems that St. John made the mistake of reading his poems to religious who persuaded him to explain them, and he explained them by writing of the only things he and they had in common, the difficulties within the life of prayer. But the dark night of the poem, while dark, is also happy (*dichosa*), a "night more lovely than the dawn." And well it might be said to be happy, for apart from any period of contemplation it was the night when St. John slid down his knotted sheets from the battlements of his prison and somehow—he did not remember how—got over the garden wall into the street beyond. "O dichosa ventura!" And even if this does not refer to his escape from prison, even if it really does refer to a contemplative experience, the darkness is still happy. The very darkness is on fire with the aching of love, yet peaceful and safe, befitting a night in which one lover is to be united with another. And this is precisely the beauty of a poem which moves readers who know nothing—and care nothing—about contemplation; it plainly describes that happy period of waiting most men and women know firsthand, waiting in the assurance that the one they love is coming and will grant them their heart's desire. Of course, this equally well describes a contemplative moment. What it does not describe is the unhappiness of the dark night of the manuals on prayer (including St. John's).

When I say it also describes a contemplative moment, I am not thinking primarily of that stage of contemplation called unitive, but rather of an aspect of the dark night

[2] *The Dark Night of the Soul*, Bk. I, ch. 8 (New York: Doubleday Image Books, 1959).
[3] *Ibid.*, Bk. II, ch. 5–6.

itself. For the originality of St. John's analysis of this night lies not so much in his confession of its horrors as in his explanation of them. The intention of his explanation is to reassure other contemplatives that they enter the dark night not because they have failed, but because they have successfully prepared themselves by "purgative" methods to let the Holy Spirit take over and finish the work they had begun. Understood this way, the dark night is God's night and therefore to be rejoiced in. Unused to getting along without the commonplace pleasures and activities of a religious life, yet all the more anxious to commune with God, the soul suffers God's mercy and loving care. The first, and normal, reaction to this passivity is bewilderment, the sense of being lost in the woods. Rightly understood, this state can be interpreted as the beginning of the highest stage of contemplation, the unitive. And this is a tranquil, a secure, and a happy state to be in, for the soul is now in good hands at last, free of struggle and self-concern. St. John's poem may well be describing the dark night from this point of view. It certainly does not tell of the grievous suffering undergone by a contemplative who does not yet realize that all is well. We might compare it to the lover waiting in the dark for someone he fears will never come, and then, unexpectedly, discovering the loved one at his side, where she had been all the time. St. John's "dark contemplation," or "dark love," may feel like a lost love to the despairing or the humble; actually, it is love found and responsive at last. St. John's intention was to confirm, as best he could, the reality of this response.

Whoever has been driven to reading his prose works, driven by the hope that they will illuminate the poems, cannot help noticing that they are largely concerned with what has been called "the negative way" to God. St. John himself accepted the threefold way which Dionysius the

114

Areopagite had outlined a thousand years earlier: " 'Three-fold is the way to God. The first is the way of purification, in which the mind is inclined to learn true wisdom. The second is the way of illumination, in which the mind by contemplation is kindled to the burning of love. The third is the way of union, in which the mind by understanding, reason, and spirit is led up by God alone.' "[4] But he departs from it in several ways. In the first place, he did not think of contemplation as intellectual (he would not have said, "the mind . . . ") but spiritual, representing the whole man. In the second place, for St. John contemplation was a progress of love. And in the third place, he would have inserted the dark night as a stage between the illuminative and the unitive. In fact, ecstasy is only a fevered, temporary, and untypical foretaste of union with God. Perhaps we can understand this better by converting the contemplative experience of ecstasy into an analogy with human love. The raptures of the man or woman first surprised by a loved one's response not only may be followed by profound depression but is not to be compared to the true joys of union, when no question can be asked about the abiding character of affection and response. St. Francis of Assisi's conviction as to the source of perfect joy is relevant here. He wanted his friars to understand that perfect joy is not experienced by healing the sick, or by foretelling the future, or by understanding the secrets of hearts or creatures. Rather, it should be likened to the friar who, standing outside a friary gate in the cold, knocks and asks to be let in; the doorkeeper rushes out with his knotted stick and belabors the poor friar, rolling him in the snow and stomping on him. The victim thinks only of the sufferings of Christ and that he must bear his own troubles for the sake of Him.

[4] Quoted in Underhill, *The Essentials of Mysticism* (New York: Dutton, 1960), p. 11.

"Write down that here is the source of perfect joy." And so does the lover, whether of God or man, wait patiently in the night, reminding himself that this is the way, already taken by mankind, and is the beginning of true joy. Patience and humility are surer signs of the constancy of true love than ecstasy, which is egocentric even when it is not delusive.

The classical terminology for the stages of contemplation is badly in need of translation into categories more suggestive of a course of love most of us are more familiar with. Indeed, the old threefold way is not above the suspicion that it is adequate only when it refers to the intellectual experience of a progressive stripping from the mind—emptying is a better word—of all objects except God (or the story of God in the life of Jesus Christ). If such is the method, then no one should be astonished to find that the objects that have been stripped away are held in contempt. In this way the existential is separated from the mystical. When the soul strains out into the infinite, the finite is left behind, not having been plumbed to its depths but just bypassed, ignored. The only similarity between this process and human love would come from the concentration of one person on another, so that as result, the rest of the world is temporarily forgotten. But this is itself only one stage in a lover's progress, and by no means the happiest or the longest. Love not only becomes blind toward the world, it sometimes does not see its intended object very well. The lover who is secure and happy in his love feels at one with a world which he thinks he is seeing in its wholeness and specific beauty for the first time as a result of his love. In any event, lovers do not enter on their course of love by deliberately putting out of mind all other human beings and all nature. While a calculating seducer lays out his course with scrupulous care, a spontaneous lover does nothing of the sort. A person in love is carried along from one stage to another. However relevant the category of "purgative" may be to love at any level, it certainly is not applicable to the beginning of love.

And perhaps it is not as relevant to man's love of God either. If one can make the effort to disassociate the interior life of a philosopher or theologian from the interior life of a man in love (with God or with man or woman)— and I strongly suggest that we make this effort—we may discover that all love begins in the same way, in a dream. It matters little whether we dream of love at night or in the daytime, whether it is a dream of longing or of meeting, whether it is a cry from the heart or a vision. To use the language of Simone Weil, we begin with consent, even before we are aware of having been questioned. The English word "want" bears the superficial ambiguity of our initial consciousness of love; we feel the lack of, and we desire. Accordingly, the beginning of love is mysterious. How can we consent to something or someone unknown? How can we lack anything or anyone unless we know someone or something is missing? St. Augustine's answer is the classical theological answer: "Our hearts are restless until they rest in You." So the human lover might reply: "I was looking for you all the time, long before I knew you existed." He did not seek until he had dreamed; he did not dream until his restless daytime soul erupted in the night. He was given the lead; it came, he did not know enough to ask for it. Call it grace, if you will, the gift of the dream, the first of several graces in the lovers' progress.

Everyone knows that dreaming does not make reality. There are persons who long in anguish all their lives for a love that never comes their way. And after a time they doubt themselves and hate a universe that is indifferent to them. They sought and they waited; their ardor oscillated between patience and impatience. They lived out their lives in the second stage of love. One day perhaps they met one whose appearance seemed to match their dream, and in this encounter they learned something of the peace and the ecstasy of association with figures in a realized landscape. Longing had not brought Beatrice to Dante. But a gift had been given, and peace and ecstasy assimilated as foretastes of greater gifts to come: a glance, a few words, a smile, a touch, an embrace, a kiss, some sign that reality differs from vision. The feelings that accompany this second grace of love are meant to be reassuring; they are often mistaken for the beginning of the end. The lover is cast into the pit when his love leaves him, and he no longer knows for sure whether she had stepped out of his dream or out of their common world. She is not there to tell him that she knows him and knows his heart. There is no more bitter moment than, after a parting, the awakening to its apparent finality. How casual are the meetings and partings of life, how like death are rejections and journeys to some other country. Why, the heart cries, should I be given so much if so much is to be taken away?

And so the way is leveled for the fifth stage of love, the doubt and self-doubt, the pain of loss and the overwhelming nostalgia, and finally the loss of trust and faith. At this point it should be obvious that there is some analogy between love's progress and the three classical stages. The dark night is the night of absence, loss, emptiness which succeeds the peak of ecstasy in the encounter with a living vision. And here too is the place where we can distinguish between the contemplative's discipline and the human lover's. The lover who has lost his beloved wallows helplessly in a sea of nostalgia and despair. If he becomes so tired, so heartsick, so cynical that he does not wish to survive, he can deliberately kill himself or the love inside him

—or it may be killed by some callous act of the one he loves. He has one other alternative, to place himself under the strictest discipline possible, to enter finally the purgative way, without hope, without faith, and without love. When this happens, he will have become a man at last, on his own and yet utterly dependent on a power which has enabled him to function freely without conscious love, faith, or hope. If there is anything at all in this analogy between the human lover and the contemplative, St. John's assurance that the Holy Spirit has taken over and true contemplation begun is at least the beginning of an explanation.

It seems to me that this is the real location for the purgative way in a progress of love and that it is confusing because it is inappropriate to try to locate it at the very beginning, for the marks of the purgative are resolution and control, not simple control. Unless the lover's spirit is willing to accept final defeat, it very much needs to resolve to go on, and in order to go to it must purify life of all that is trivial or distracting.

> Endeavor to be inclined always:
> not to the easiest, but to the most difficult,
> not to the most delightful, but to the harshest,
> not to wanting something, but to wanting nothing,
> and desire to enter into complete nudity, emptiness, and
>   poverty in everything in the world.[5]

This is what T. S. Eliot called "the inner freedom from the practical desire," and which he spelled out in his summary of St. John's directions accompanying his sketch of the ascent of Mt. Carmel. St. John had said, in part,

> To come to the pleasure you have not
> you must go by a way in which you enjoy not

---

[5] St. John of the Cross, *The Spiritual Canticle* in *The Collected Works of St. John of the Cross*, pp. 102–3.

To come to the knowledge you have not
you must go by a way in which you know not
To come to the possession you have not
you must go by a way in which you possess not
To come to be what you are not
you must go by a way in which you are not.[6]

And Eliot:

In order to arrive there,
To arrive where you are, to get from where you are not,
You must go by a way wherein there is no ecstasy.
In order to arrive at what you do not know
You must go by a way which is the way of ignorance
In order to possess what you do not possess
You must go by the way of dispossession.
In order to arrive at what you are not
You must go through the way in which you are not
And what you do not know is the only thing you know
And what you own is what you do not own
And where you are is where you are not.[7]

The "way wherein there is no ecstasy" is beyond the romantic dream, beyond even ecstasy itself. It is the way of survival after ecstasy, and particularly after the loss of the dreamed-of loved one. It may be understood, of course, as the way of preparation for philosophic wisdom; perhaps St. John himself also had this in mind. But its achievement can be seen in the disciplined verses of his poetry. Their limpid surface only conceals a mastering of all that is essential to total vision and total reception of the beloved's unexpected return. "Now that I no longer desire . . . I have them all . . . without desire."[8] Lest it be thought that the avoidance of the trivial and the distracting is an inferior task after ecstasy and its accompanying tranquillity, I would urge that we remember it is quite possible to have rapturous

---

[6] *Ibid.*, p. 67.
[7] "East Coker," *Four Quartets* (New York: Harcourt Brace, 1943), p. 51.
[8] St. John of the Cross, *The Spiritual Canticle.*

experiences without the prior benefit of self-discipline. In other words, there is no necessary order which requires that the purgative precede the illuminative way. One may suspect that even the greatest manuals of prayer are at times prescriptive rather than descriptive.

It is probably natural that anyone knowing the special happiness of ecstasy, "standing outside" his ordinary self and feelings, should find it difficult to return to them afterwards without disdain. That he should want to continue voluntarily the privilege of concentrated vision and feeling, momentarily and involuntarily experienced, is to be expected. And if he chooses not to surrender his integrity when he finds no more gifts and graces, he at least has the best motive for entering upon a life of self-discipline. This exercise will not have as its aim the survival of self-respect only, but will find its self-respect in the new understanding of reality that grows with the perfecting of its power to see and feel. There is a place for asceticism of this sort in existential as well as in mystical love. In fact, we may be more sure of its place within the spiritual structure of experience once we have seen the whole sequence of human loving.

I am suggesting that instead of accepting as settled fact a spiritual sequence in which the purgative is followed by the illuminative (or ecstatic), and that in turn is succeeded by the dark night and the unitive, we consider the location of the purgative as part of the rather complex experience of the dark night. I would say more. The purgative, unless it is only an empty display of ascetic skill for the sake of skill, and buttressed by a sick contempt for its own past, will contain within it a hidden power that may in time bring it consenting to the unitive state. That power is longing, a purified longing, no longer romantic and visionary, subject to illusions, but compounded of natural desire and a sense of fate. Such is the significance of St. John's *Stanzas of the Soul That Suffers with Longing to See God*.

> I no longer live within myself
> And I cannot live without God,
> For if I have neither Him nor myself
> What will life be?
> It will be a thousand deaths,
> Longing for my true life
> And dying because I do not die.

We could see these and the verses that follow them as imitations of St. Teresa's "I die because I do not die." But we would be wrong. Compare the complacency of "For now I live a life unseen,"[9] with St. John's

> "This life that I live is no life at all,"
> A fish that leaves the water
> Has this relief:
> The dying it endures
> Ends at last in death.
> What death can equal
> My pitiable life?
> For the longer I live, the more drawn out is my dying.

To compare them is to recognize the threefold nature of St. John's dark night, compounded of separation, longing, and candor. St. John had heard the secular lyric of the streets that ended with the line, "I am dying of love, dearest, what shall I do?—Die." Probably St. Teresa had heard it too. And he had this in his ears when he wrote, "I will cry out for death." He was dying of love, "since I do not see You as I desire," dying "until I live with You." We have only to compare this with Heathcliff's longing for death in *Wuthering Heights* to realize that St. John's leading theme is not a devaluation of the world but an inability to imagine the world apart from its true center, God (for

[9] *The Complete Works of St. Teresa of Jesus*, trans. E. Allison Peers (New York: Sheed and Ward, 1946), III, 277.

Heathcliff, Cathy). In Him is comprehended all that is real, in Him is life.

This may be the end of the line, for the mystical as well as the existential. On this earth there are only two more possible stages, and there is no guarantee that they will be experienced. For this too grace is needed, and, if we can believe the theologians, although there is sufficient grace for each of us, each of us may not need the same kind. This is a way perhaps of putting a good face on the fact that a man can die without arriving at the unitive stage. There may be no return, no second chance, no second encounter, and therefore no fullness of joy, no joy at all. It is possible to go through life and know no ecstasy; it is just as possible to go through life and not know the difference between ecstasy and joy. This is what Dionysius had in mind, no doubt, when he remarked that real union is beyond ecstasy—by definition—and that the soul will experience changes in personality as well as moral effects. The pulsating self-pity, anger, depression of the first impact of the dark night will have vanished for good. Above all, love will prevail, enough for everyone. For how long? So long as life lasts, until the second absence, the new parting. One lover dies before the other, yet their union leaves a sacramental power that is kept going by love of the unseen. And so man loves God the unseen because he was once loved by the seen. We love because someone first loved us. And man's love at the end of his spiritual adventures is enough for everyone, the unseen as well as the seen. "O dichosa ventura!"

It is likely that the less a person knows about the classical scheme of contemplation the more likely he will be able to understand St. John's poem *The Dark Night of the Soul*. And it is a waste of time to try to fit his other major poems into that threefold way; they do not fit. Indeed, even though they may all be thought of as describing aspects of the unitive life, the more I read them the more I wonder whether we do not make a mistake at all times in conceiving the stages as a kind of horizontal, chronological scheme. For someone like St. John, and for anyone whose life is defined by love, the scheme, if there is any, might better be described vertically. In this way it is possible to relate *Stanzas Concerning an Ecstasy, The Dark Night, Stanzas of the Soul That Suffers with Longing,* and *The Spiritual Canticle* to one stage only of St. John's life, whatever one may call it. They do not represent, any or all of them, stages that he had surpassed, or could surpass. And so we find it necessary to revise the meaning of "dark night," "ecstasy," "longing" to bring them in line with the life he was living when he wrote the *Canticle.* St. Augustine's plea "Give me a lover and he will understand what I mean" is especially relevant to the reading of St. John of the Cross. And it does not matter if the lover is existential rather than mystical. Perhaps it does matter, perhaps it is safer. As St. John himself said, "The stanzas were obviously composed with a certain burning love of God. . . . It would be foolish to think that expressions of love arising from mystical understanding, like these stanzas, are fully explainable."[10] It may be equally foolish to assume that expressions of love arising in any other way are explainable either. But we can try.

We know that St. John of the Cross liked to listen to the popular love songs of his day; he even enjoyed singing them. But above all he loved the Song of Songs. And on his deathbed he asked one of the brothers to read some verses from the Song. And as he heard them he murmured, "O que preciosas margaritas!" Who can tell what he heard in them? It is doubtful that he heard only the hardlined figurative theology of St. Bernard. Of course, it is

---

[10] *The Collected Works of St. John of the Cross,* p. 408.

124

easy to do St. Bernard an injustice since we have not inherited any homely little stories about him that might soften the edges of his high-minded disdain of the lovely things of this world. We know enough of St. John to be assured that however profound his contemplative life, it was not protected by contempt. He would go off by himself to a church tower, a grotto in a garden, a cave on a hilltop, and gaze out through the opening at the landscape below. There he would contemplate. He loved the mountains and the valleys that made up the panorama. There come to mind the several passages in Stendhal's novels in which Julien Sorel on a mountaintop, Fabrice del Dongo in a tower by Lake Como also looked out over the countryside and refreshed their souls. This characteristic and necessary affection for landscape is particularly noticeable in *The Spiritual Canticle*. Indeed, a reading of the text unbiased by the rules of mystical theology could disclose much that should be obvious.

If the first thing to remark on is that this poem is in some way modeled on the Song of Songs and, in fact, is entitled a "spiritual" song, the second thing to observe is that the imagery of the model is not as predominant as St. John's own imagery. There are thirty-nine (forty in the Codex of Jaen) stanzas of five lines each, arranged as a duet between Bride and Bridegroom. Differences appear at once. Although the Bride once tended a herd, and could be considered a shepherdess, her beloved is likened to a stag, and the general imagery of the poem is of a hunt rather than an adoration. It is a pastoral poem mainly because of the references to landscape rather than occupation. The Song of Songs is dominated by the series of encomiums of the Bride's beauty. Only once in the *Canticle* is her beauty mentioned, and then only as a reflection of the beauty of her beloved. There are no lengthy praises of the beloved's beauty; instead it is reflected in the world of nature. Both poems begin with longing, but whereas the Song's longing never ends, and in fact becomes more intense, especially in night dreams, the mood of the *Canticle* soon shifts, as the sought-for beloved returns to stay.

There is a special pleasure in the occasional borrowing of imagery from the older poem: "tell him," "north-wind," "return," "garden," "under the apple tree," "messengers," "lost-found," "dark beauty," "foxes," "vineyard," "roses," "south-wind," "fears of night," "girls of Judea," "Aminadab." But the pleasure arises from their relative unimportance, as the lightest notes of a light counterpoint in the background. In the foreground of St. John's poem is a longing that suffers unto death, that bears a wound from the touching of the departed lover. And the loved one has fled and gone into hiding, leaving the lover alone, stammering, begging to be healed. In his absence all creation witnesses to his beauty; when he returns all creation rejoices in its fullness. To read this poem is to meet an original work of love, depending no more on the older poem than Shakespeare's *Hamlet* does on older plays.

The Song of Songs is egocentric from the beginning, and its luxuriance befits self-adulatory longing. *The Spiritual Canticle* is much more direct in its preoccupation with the hidden God. "Where?" "You fled." "I went out calling You." "Tell me, has He passed by you?" In His absence the soul will "sicken, suffer, and die." This lovesickness is unto death. Without Him man cannot live; if He remains in hiding man will gradually die. And so the soul seeks Him, heads for the mountains (Mt. Carmel, "that high state of perfection we call union of a soul with God"),[11] the mountains of Toledo seen from his prison cell. On his way to the mountains he passes through meadows in

[11] *Ibid.*, p. 69.

flower and then the olive and scrub on the hillsides. The hidden God has already passed through them all, and they are beautiful in his image, but it is a beauty that hurts; it reminds the soul of the original beauty of the creator.

> All wound me more
> And leave me dying
> Of, ah, I-don't-know-what behind their stammering.
> *Un no se que que quedan balbuciendo*

Just so a man in love with a woman, "brought near death by the sorrows you receive," like St. Teresa receiving the stigmatum of the angel's spear, feels the loved one's touch long after she has gone. And having had all he could do to keep from touching her for so long, once touched by her he can never recover his primal innocence.

> How do you endure
> O life, not living where you live?

While we do not easily forget the sensuousness of the Song of Songs, and especially its opening yearning for the kisses of the beloved, it is in St. John's poem rather that the beloved touches, wounds, disappears, returns, and holds the lover's head in his arms. Except for the humble and tranquil resting on the breast and in the arms of the beloved, the wounding comes from the eyes—the recognition—of the beloved. To be seen by the man she loves is sweet hurt enough, to rest on him the farthest reach of her desire. St. John is not sensual, but then neither is all existential love. He knew in his own way how little a lover wants, how little it takes to satisfy. "The eyes I have desired,/Which I bear sketched deep within my heart" are the first response of love, and their own vision of beauty, imprinted in the one they look at, is an almost unbearable pain. This is the pain of the creature realizing for the first time that it is a creature, finite, in want of its life. To know what one is missing feels far worse than never to know at all. In Sophocles' *King Oedipus* the play on "eyes" is a play on sight and blindness, wisdom and ignorance; in *The Spiritual Canticle* it is hard not to feel that St. John was one of those people (Dostoevsky may have been another) who, when he sees another person, sees only his eyes. For him eyes are the heart and soul of the person they look out from. They speak, they touch, they love. As he was to say a few years later in "The Living Flame of Love," when they touch, they "tenderly wound my soul in its deepest center. . . . O sweet cautery, O delightful wound! How gently and lovingly you wake in my heart, where in secret You dwell alone . . . and swell my heart with love."

And so it comes about that we can speak of the dominant imagery of this poem as imagery of reflection:

> When You looked at me
> Your eyes imprinted Your grace in me . . .
> And thus my eyes deserved
> To adore what they beheld in You.

Instead of saying, "We love because he first loved us," St. John might have said "We see because he has first seen us." And what we see is the origin of what we see with. Therefore, the lover claims in gratitude, "Now I can see because you once showed me how; I see with your eyes." We who are in love learn to see the world through each other's eyes; and all we require to see is to remember the beloved by name. There are no passages more important than stanzas 13 and 14 (Codex Sanlucar), and they should be translated literally:

> My beloved, the mountains,
> the lonely wooded valleys,
> the strange islands,
> the resounding rivers,
> the whistling of amorous breezes,

the quiet night,
at the rising of the dawn,
the hushed music,
the resounding solitude,
the supper that refreshes and makes one love the more.

To invoke the eyes, the image, the name of the one she loves is to invoke everything in the world that they both love, and love together. For St. John it is a world of mountains, valleys, strange islands, breezes on the hilltop, the night, the dawn, and above all quiet and solitude. The only human element is the supper, perhaps even the sacramental supper of Holy Communion. Is this not "the sweet living knowledge" that he had learned "in the inner wine cellar [bodega]"? Was St. John's experience so unitary that in the end the songs of love from the wine cellar he heard as he walked by in the street above impressed him as deeply as the lines from the eucharistic meal intoned in the convent chapel? I recall a story of a priest on the run in Spain during the civil war who, in desperation and in love, celebrated mass with glass of wine and crust of bread as he sat with a companion at a wooden table in a Madrid bodega. If the world is one, why then should not mass be offered (as Teilhard de Chardin believed) on "the altar of the world"? Why should not living knowledge be heard from a wine cellar? Why should not the mystical be existential?

The Spiritual Canticle is not a nostalgic dream but a joyous remembrance. How gently he mentions "watching fears of night," compared to the two dramatic dream sequences of the Song of Songs, with their poignancy and pathos; fears such as these form, along with birds, stags, mountains, winds, ardors, elements with which God casts a spell on the world so that the one he loves may sleep "in deeper peace." And the poem moves rapidly, lightly, in

129

complete trust over the remembrance of this great love affair.

> Nor have I any other work
> Now that my every act is love.

The Prodigal Son left home of his own free will; in this poem it is the stag having fled who left the wounded soul behind. In love she is lost, and then found. To this extent the poem comprehends the two encounters within the seven stages of love. The great lover returns, and by returning redeems (as Christ on the cross) the exiled children of Eve, "beneath the apple tree." And, as Lady Julian said, "All shall be well, all manner of thing shall be well." So much in love, mindful of the beloved's healing touch, the lover is willing to live by herself, needing no one else. For his sake she lives alone. And for her sake the beloved compassionately takes up the burden of solitude and guides her in it. "He does not wish to leave her alone." Even solitude cannot separate lovers, for if they endure the solitude for one another, they will rejoice in one another's care.

The last stanzas of the poem describe the nature of the joy that is beyond solitude, especially the solitude that is sacrificial. Once again it is necessary to translate literally, for even St. John's commentary—almost poetic at this point —does not, I think, tell the characteristic truth of his understanding of love. Stanza 35 (Codex Sanlucar) should read:

> Let us rejoice, Beloved,
> And let us go forth to behold in your beauty,
> to the mountain and to the hill. . . .

Most translations insert "ourselves" between "behold" and "in your beauty." St. John himself does in his commentary: "This means: Let us so act that by means of this loving activity we may attain to a vision of ourselves in Your

130

beauty in eternal love. That is: That I be so transformed
in Your beauty that we may be alike in beauty, and behold
ourselves in Your beauty. . . . I shall see You in Your
beauty, and You shall see me in Your beauty, and I shall
see myself in Your beauty, and You will see Yourself in me
in Your beauty. . . ."[12] And no doubt the lovers do see
each other in each other's beauty. But the basic effect of
their being together is simply that they are able to *see*, and
to see through the beauty of the one who loved first. And
they will see much more than each other; through love the
whole world can be known. For St. John himself loved
his Spanish landscape more than he loved any single man
or woman in it. And where for another man the effect of
loving God and being loved by Him would be love of the
neighbor, for St. John the effect is to have his natural love
of the natural world validated.

Now he knew he was right in climbing into the tower,
ascending the hillsides to the caves at the summits, "to the
high caverns in the rock which are so well concealed."
There he would sit, there he would love God, with God
returning love, there would he gaze out over the plains, and

> There You will show me
> What my soul has been seeking,
> And then You will give me,
> You, my life, will give me there
> What You gave me on that other day:

All that he had ever wanted to see could now be seen, all
that he had ever sought had now been found, all that he
had given "on that other day," the first time they met,
"You, my life," now will give forever. What You gave
then, You give again:

> The breathing of the air
> (breathing with God's own love)

---

[12] *Ibid.*, p. 547.

The song of the sweet nightingale,
(God's voice saying, "Arise, make haste, my love, my dove,
my beautiful one, and come; for now the winter has
        passed . . .)
The grove and its living beauty,
(grace, wisdom, and beauty)
In the serene night,
(in contemplation, the secret, hidden knowledge of God)
With a flame that is consuming and painless.
(the love of the Holy Spirit)

I have inserted in parentheses lines from St. John's commentary because this juxtaposition shows more clearly than any explanation the composition of his mind. St. John of the Cross did not use the imagery of the Spanish landscape in order to conceal his religious life, which he later made explicit in commentaries. He wrote poems and used natural pictures because he loved song and loved the world about which he sang. He associated religious contemplation with the world and sought that world whenever he wanted to remember God. God taught him to see that world, and in that world he had learned to know God. The two were inseparable. The commentaries tell only part of the story of his mind; had he written no poetry we should be justified in supposing that that one part was all the mind he had, a mystical as opposed to an existential mind. His poems not only show the other part of his mind; they are beautiful enough, because they are symbolic, to comprehend them both.

The last stanza may seem obscure, but for me it is as moving as any in the poem. St. John did not indicate that it is not spoken by the Bride, but it seems obvious to me that it is a choral ending.

> No one looked at her,
> Nor did Aminadab appear;
> The siege was still;

> And the cavalry,
> At the sight of the waters descended.

After the images of silence and the reminder of a love that burns but does not hurt because it is a careful love, all is safe. Not even Aminadab—Satan—will turn up. Temptations no longer assail. All troubles recede in the distant past as the cavalry winds down the road toward the river crossing.

13.

PASSION AND SEPARATION

TO SOME it might appear that there are two parallel ways of thinking about love, discursively and symbolically. Both ways are possible, and perhaps both should be employed. But they are not parallel. That is, one is not as good as the other, one to be preferred to the other according to the temperament of the person using it. There is no question that some men are more given to abstractions, some to poetry. But we do not learn as much about love from philosophers and theologians as from poets and novelists. The reason is simple, and it is the same reason that we do not learn as much from philosophy and theology as from our own personal experience: too much is left out. The philosopher does not exhaust experience in his attempt to reduce it to its essentials; he leaves behind that which he cannot deal with. I do not have in mind only those philosophers and theologians who do not even seem interested in love, but rather those who are moved by their conviction of the primacy of love to want to state its message, its dynamism and its purpose, its origin and its effects. The immediacy, or better, the urgency of love cannot easily be conveyed discursively: the two modes are opposed. And since the primacy of love depends on the urgency, it is not surprising that the discursive mode sometimes fails to convince even those with the best of intentions.

There is another reason why symbolic expressions of love are needed. Perhaps symbolism is inherently more convincing, and more profound. Although we do and must understand in universal terms even those things which are most personal and individual to us, we understand them best by analogy rather than by abstraction. For analogy does not let us forget an important feature of our experience, namely that everything we do, and more especially the purest and most fundamental of our passions, connects us with the rest of creation. This is the rightness of the magnificent sequences of adoration in the Song of Songs. A man can say to a girl, "You are beautiful," but she will not know how beautiful, and therefore how much he loves her, if he cannot connect her beauty with the beauty of all the world. She is like this, and like that. Even so, of course, her beauty is not exhausted, but the very totality of allusion reminds us of that. She does not exist in a vacuum. Indeed, because she does not, loving her enables the man to love the world as well. Lonely without her, he discovers the world and communion through her.

In addition to the comparing of a loved one to other parts of the cosmos, there is an analogy between one love and another. And in the search for the essence of one love affair, as distinct from others, the mind falls back on analogies to other love affairs. What person who has been in love does not know the embarrassment of discovering himself uttering endearments that can only be called cliches? Yet they sound right for the occasion and the person. Who has not discovered, or fancied he has discovered, striking similarities between his love affair and, let us say, Heloise and Abelard, or Launcelot and Gwynevere? To see a similarity is almost to provide an explanation, if not justification, for whatever is questionable or original. A relatively small number of lovers, some legendary and some real, form a store of exemplars on which all philosophically minded lovers can draw for their poetic sustenance. For it is true that in a sense the motive behind the use of allusion is philosophical: we would try to peg down the essence of the individual situation.

We should not find it strange, therefore, that just as each of us may try to relate his own love to other and grander affairs, so some of us should invent a love affair in order to understand our own. This is the symbolic necessity behind some of the stories of love that are themselves taken as exemplary today. If the Song of Songs has always been a paradigm for mystical and existential lovers, it may have been also for the person who wrote it. Even if it tells a much more literal story of wooing, betrothal, marriage than we can be sure of, it is a record of one person's rhythm of love—in musical form, so to speak—that should be taken as the only way he himself had to explain himself to himself. And we cannot point to any discursive treatments of love, whether in Plato or St. Thomas Aquinas, that lead us both sympathetically and undeviatingly to the shape of existential love as we know it. If St. Bernard and others are right, and the Song of Songs was intended from the outset to be read figuratively (or should be) this proposition would still hold good. Mystical love can be fully understood only in the context of existential love, not because the existential is more familiar—to some it was not—but because the mystical is the pure spirit blowing through the existential.

St. John of the Cross presents another variation of the use of symbolism. His *Spiritual Canticle* makes use of some of the imagery of the Song of Songs, primarily the dialogue form. In fact, the second word in his title, *Canticle*, alone would be sufficient to recall the whole original. And yet in spite of the first word, *Spiritual*, he does not refer to God or to Christ anywhere in the poem. It may be said that he did not need to, because by his time the figurative mode of

137

interpretation was so well established, But that is not all. A reading of the poem will show that in St. John's mind there is a fusion of earth and spirit so constant, so strong, that we may suspect that he himself did not realize its meaning. In any event, we can agree not only that he wrote the poem before he wrote the commentary, but that his poetic treatment of love was the way he chose to retain for himself the most vivid sense of his experience. And if the poem suggests to us more than he ever admitted to knowing, it is quite possible that he experienced more than he could say, except in poetry.

If the mystery of St. John of the Cross was in some measure unknown to himself except through the symbolism of his poetry, what are we to think of Emily Brontë's *Wuthering Heights?* By all standards the most passionate love story in English literature, it was written by a girl of twenty-eight who had never been in love. And there is no reason to think that she meant it to be read figuratively as the story of man's love with God. Indeed, the most elementary comparison between this story and all one has heard of man's love for God and God's for man would make such a hypothesis look ridiculous. Passion certainly abounds in the relationship between the human and the divine: love, and also jealousy, anger, sorrow. There is quite as much storm as peace between man and God. But how could anyone for a minute seriously think of either Catherine Earnshaw or Heathcliff as a symbol for God? It never occurred to either of them to say that the other is perfect: neither worshiped the other as inferior to superior. In this sense, courtly love was a fair figure for religious love. But Heathcliff is not a courtly lover. A case could be made for the resemblance of Cathy to Queen Gwynevere, imperious, changeable, unkind. And Cathy, for all she says of her identity with Heathcliff, does not worship him. On the

contrary, no one in the novel lists his unlovely characteristics more frankly.

But to say that *Wuthering Heights* is not a figure for a
biblical kind of love does not mean that we cannot associate
it with religion in any way. This association has been made,
and very persuasively, by Derek Traversi, whose view is that
the story is about a metaphysical passion for completion
which is religious in nature.[1] To say it is metaphysical
might be thought enough, without adding "religious."
Yet Emily Brontë narrates a tale of passionate love so pure
that we can see once and for all the nature of this passion.
This is why it has become exemplary for us. If it is its
purity which makes it metaphysical, it is the goal of the
passion that permits us to call it religious. God is not part
of the story itself, but the desire for completion of one life
in another is a desire which, so far as the story is concerned,
is doomed not to be fulfilled. Whether it is—or can be—
fulfilled at all, beyond time and in eternity, is another
matter resolved in the book only in the mind of the dying
Heathcliff, but not assured us by the novelist herself in
any other way. Granted Emily Brontë's own religious
orthodoxy, it seems to me permissible to wonder whether,
even for her, Heathcliff's longing was not delusive. There
is no life in the grave.

If Emily Brontë's story is not the figure of her own existential love (transitive, with some real man in the background)
or her own mystical love (transitive, with God in the foreground), what was it a figure for? Surely this story is a
figure of something. How could it have been written at
all? From what order of experience did it come? There can
be, it seems to me, no definitive answer to this. Here we
touch on one of the mysteries of the human personality.

---

[1] "The Brontë Sisters and *Wuthering Heights*," *The Pelican Guide to English
Literature*, ed. Boris Ford (Baltimore: Penguin, 1963), Vol. 6, pp. 256–74.

Like Traversi I, too, can only guess and hope that my own reading of the text may confirm to some extent the direction of my guesses. At the outset there comes to mind the possibility of a comparison between Emily Brontë's spiritual thrust and that which Rilke, writing of Abelone's singing, defines as non-transitive. But this would mean that Emily Brontë was using a transitive love as image of a non-transitive love. That would not be impossible. The very intensity of Heathcliff's passion for Cathy, alive and dead, can be isolated for examination, but only by doing violence to its indissoluble connection with Cathy. This is what Traversi is thinking of when he discourages us from looking at the novel as one more example of romanticism and points out that romantic sentiment is characterized by its self-centeredness. Now no one could pretend that in one sense of the word Heathcliff is not self-centered, i.e., he does not care what happens to other people, including Cathy on her deathbed. But he does care for Cathy, and his passion makes no sense at all except as love for *her*. To try to maintain, therefore, that the novel is a figure for non-transitive love in the heart of Emily Brontë is to miss the point, namely, that even without having a real lover she knew that this was the only thing worth having.

Is that so difficult to understand? To paraphrase St. Augustine, how are we to know we have arrived, unless we have been there before? There is something about human nature which is not satisfied until it completes itself in another person. Emily Brontë says all this in her story. Does she say more? Does she say that only in death, or not even in death, is this kind of fulfillment possible? Many mystics would say the latter, and some of them would say so, no doubt, because they had despaired of good fortune in this life. Others perhaps were more independently convinced, by the mystical tradition in which they grew up, for most of the mystics began their religious life early, in their teens, before anyone has the right to pronounce on his chances. It seems to me that there is an open critical question as to whether the image of death that many have observed to be hovering over this novel is at the end full of hope or of pathos. What is clearer, however, is the angry frustration of Heathcliff from the beginning until near the end. Frustration and longing combined are recognizable comparisons in the life of one who wants but cannot have. And when we remember that in an obvious way this novel is asexual as well, that the lovers are never alone long enough to go to bed together (perhaps the very thought may seem indecent), we should more than wonder why the yearning is so shot through with anger and impatience.

Yet while it is true that this existential passion does not complete itself in sexual intercourse, it is a sexual passion. Anyone who is tempted to say that Cathy could have spoken Heathcliff's lines, and he her lines, would soon have to reject the notion. The lines are not interchangeable, nor do they make a composite figure, their creator Emily Brontë. On the contrary, she had imagined through Heathcliff a masculine desire for presence, exasperated and lonely, and in Catherine Earnshaw, a feminine assurance of identity. It is hardly possible to think of Heathcliff's saying, "I am Cathy," without smiling, and not because we have heard Cathy's "I am Heathcliff" all our lives. Men do not often feel this way about women, but many women do about men, and men often fear this as a form of possession. This is why it is not inconsistent for Cathy to say she wants to die, even though this would mean leaving Heathcliff at the very moment when he has been reunited with her. That last scene in her bedroom frustrates masculine pride but is perfectly plausible from a woman's point of view: " 'Oh, you see, Nelly, he would not relent a moment to keep me out of the grave. *That* is how I'm loved! Well, never mind. That is not *my* Heathcliff. I shall love mine yet; and take him with me—he's in my soul. And, the thing that irks me most is this shattered prison, after all. I'm tired, tired of being enclosed here. I'm wearying to escape into that glorious world, and to be always there: not seeing it dimly through tears, and yearning for it through the walls of an aching heart, but really with it and in it.' "[2] Compare this with the passages at the end of Heathcliff's life when he too looks forward to death, but for a different reason: " 'I have to remind myself to breathe —almost remind my heart to beat. . . . I have a single wish, and my whole being and faculties are yearning to attain it. They have yearned towards it so long, and so unwaveringly, that I'm convinced it *will* be reached—and soon—because it has devoured my existence. . . . . O, God! It is a long fight. I wish it were over![3]

. . . .

Last night, I was on the threshold of hell. Today, I am within sight of my heaven. I have my eyes on it, hardly three feet to sever me!' "[4] Apart from the appropriateness of the epithets "morbid" and "macabre" to Cathy's and later Heathcliff's death wish, the contrast between them is initially shocking. This is the woman who as a child had announced so plausibly to Nelly that she would be so miserable in heaven that she would make the angels angry enough to fling her out and down onto Wuthering Heights. Its eloquence makes it worthy of a jealously existential attitude which freezes at the very mention of heaven. But it is hardly consistent with the dying woman's wish to go to "that glorious world." And even when we excuse her by

[2] Emily Brontë, *Wuthering Heights* (New York: Signet, 1962), p. 157.
[3] *Ibid.*, p. 308.
[4] *Ibid.*, p. 311.

remembering her illness, and above all the intolerable tension of her life stemming from her decision to compromise between what Edgar could give her and what Heathcliff meant to her, it is also inconsistent with her protestations of love for Heathcliff.

Longing to escape "this shattered prison"—which Heathcliff shares with her—she would go elsewhere, carrying an ideal Heathcliff (" 'He's in my soul' ") within her. But Heathcliff, dying of no known disease, only of love, yearns to escape to a dreadul solitude in which her ghostly presence torments him, in order to be re-united with her corpse in the earth. It is not easy to say which one has the better part. The difference between them, however, is marked, and I would call it a sexual difference. She takes their identity for granted, so much that she is quite willing to leave the living, carnal Heathcliff. He wants her presence so despairingly that he is willing to embrace it in the only way he can imagine possible, in a coffin. So, in fact, did Heloise imagine that she could be re-united with Peter Abelard. Could Emily Brontë have read their story?

Almost everything that either Cathy or Heathcliff says is exaggerated, or at least sounds exaggerated to anyone not in love. And almost everything is typical of someone in love. More than that, Emily Brontë's achievement was that she has said better than anyone else, even Heloise, exactly what people in love do feel, so well that they now find themselves plagiarizing because they can do no better. Although it is Cathy who says it, Heathcliff too could have said, "My great thought in living is [her] self." But her thought was of identity with him, his of longing for her. There is a difference. " 'My love for Heathcliff resembles the eternal rocks beneath—a source of little visible delight, but necessary. Nelly, I am Heathcliff! He's always, always in my mind—not as a pleasure, any more than I am

always a pleasure to myself, but as my own being. So don't
talk of our separation again; it is impracticable.' "[5] The
definition of this woman is her love for this man. The
definition of Cathy is Heathcliff, the kind of person he is.
So she says. Yet part of the pathos of her life is her attrac-
tion to Edgar Linton and all he seems to stand for: civiliza-
tion and tranquillity. And if we would dispose of Edgar by
recalling him and his sister as spoiled and pettish children,
we should also remember that as a man he had much to put
up with and ended his life with a certain dignity. Perhaps
it would be misleading to say that she is to be defined also
by her love for Edgar; it defines her pathos, not her being.
This is the significance of the other, literally nonsensical,
assertion, "He's more myself than I am." In the Sartrian
sense "her existence precedes her essence"—her love for
Heathcliff is more important than her choice of Linton as a
husband.

Nevertheless, her love for him is in some measure self-
centered. We cannot charge unambiguously that her feelings are their own justification. Yet she does not fully
consider Heathcliff's. When Nelly tells her that Heathcliff
will feel deserted once she has married Edgar, she replies
to this reasonable warning: " 'He quite deserted! We
separated!' she exclaimed, with an accent of indignation.
'Who is to separate us, pray? . . . Every Linton on the face
of the earth might melt into nothing, before I could consent to forsake Heathcliff. . . . He'll be as much to me as he
has been all his lifetime.' "[6] In real life one could only gasp
at the unreality, to say nothing of the self-centeredness of
this. To tell the truth, it is not unknown in real life. The
more one reads this novel, the more amazing her prescience
appears. But even as we settle down to condemning Cathy,
we do not escape easily the mystical reverberation of her

[5] *Ibid.*, p. 84.   [6] *Ibid.*, p. 83.

144

rhetorical question, " 'Who is to separate us?' "—"Who shall separate us from the love of Christ? Shall tribulation, or distress, or persecution, or famine, or nakedness, or peril, or sword? . . . No, in all these things we are more than conquerors through him who loved us. For I am sure that neither death, nor life, nor angels, nor principalities, nor things present, nor things to come, nor powers, nor height, nor depth, nor anything else in all creation will be able to separate us from the love of God in Christ Jesus our Lord."[7] If this seems to make too much of the verb "separate," because Christ's proximity to man is in the nature of a participation in human suffering by way of his own blood sacrifice, while Cathy is close to Heathcliff by way of assumption of a likeness, it is not wholly irrelevant. Perhaps Cathy is as unworthy of Heathcliff's love as man is of Christ's. Certainly Heathcliff is not prepared to sacrifice anything of himself and is only too willing to sacrifice his son, Linton. On reflection, however, there is a significant and profound likeness. Christ is the head of the body of which all Christians are members, as Heathcliff is "the being" of Catherine Earnshaw. And so even when she dies she is not totally separated from Heathcliff, but torments him with her separated ghostly presence. " 'She has disturbed me night and day, through eighteen years.' " She is his body. And it is no wonder that he feels he has to complete himself by having his body laid side by side with hers.

It is not enough simply to call this part of the story a demonstration of the tragic loneliness of lost or deserted love. The poignancy of the loss is in proportion to the nature of that love. Heathcliff could ask, " 'What kind of living will it be?' " for him when Cathy is dead, only because he had already asked, " 'Why did you betray your

[7] St. Paul's Epistle to the Romans 8:35–39.

own heart?' " He knew that this separation, of body from soul, being, heart, would make him frustrated and restless until the two could be brought together again. At her death he prayed that she would not rest as long as he lived, but would " 'wake in torment' ": " 'Be with me always— take any form—drive me mad! only do not leave me in this abyss, where I cannot find you. . . . I cannot live without my life. I cannot live without my soul.' "[8] This is not a case of one half of the soul looking for the other, *dimidium animae meae*, but rather of the emotional fusion of two persons who love each other so much that they cannot imagine life endurable with one dead. The purpose of living would have been canceled out. And so Heathcliff is presented the very situation which Cathy had envisaged, when as a child she had told Nelly: " 'If all else perished, and *he* remained, I should still continue to be; and all else remained, and he were annihilated, the universe would turn to a mighty stranger; I should not seem a part of it.' "[9] It is he who remains, and she still continues to be, a spiritual torment to him. She is annihilated, and the universe seems " 'a mighty stranger,' " to the extent that he is indifferent to everyone in it and waits for the day when he will rejoin her. But this is not strictly and completely true. He may not be part of the world, yet it is not entirely strange to him. On the contrary: " 'For what is not connected with her to me? and what does not recall her? I cannot look down to this floor, but her features are shaped on the flags! In every cloud, in every tree—filling the air at night, and caught by glimpses in every object, by day I am surrounded with her image! The most ordinary faces of men, and women—my own features mock me with a resemblance. . . . The world is a dreadful collection of mem-

---

[8] Brontë, *Wuthering Heights*, p. 164.   [9] *Ibid.*, p. 84.

146

oranda that she did exist and that I have lost her.' "[10] How exactly Emily Brontë has caught the photographic hang-over of the deserted lover. He finds traces of his lost love everywhere he goes. Unlikely faces remind him of the one face, voices of the one voice; the lost love is inescapable. It is as if the world witnesses in its diverse reminders to the perfection of the love he once thought unique.

Each memorandum invokes the lost presence, but only momentarily, and the result of the disillusionment is weariness with living. A little more stuffing comes out each time. Something like this could have happened to Heath-cliff, but it did not. He keeps all his stuffing right up to the end. He is not dismayed by Nelly's telling him that no-body loved him. How could that matter? It was Cathy alone he cared for, and he never doubted where her heart really lay, in life or in death. The closer to death, and her grave, he came, the more others noticed "a strange joyful glitter in his eyes." He himself said, " 'My soul's bliss kills my body, but does not satisfy itself.' "[11] Longing, when accompanied by hope, can come as near joy as a facsimile to something authentic. But longing does not bear fulfill-ment within itself, only a foretaste of it. Joy is distinguished from ecstasy, as tranquillity is distinguished from a strain-ing out to the infinite. Perhaps in spite of a slight confusion of terms, Catherine Linton's description of the difference between her idea of happiness and Linton Heathcliff's was itself a forecast of the paradisal conclusion of the novel.

> "He said the pleasantest manner of spending a hot July day was lying from morning till evening on a bank of heath in the middle of the moors, with the bees humming dreamily about among the bloom, and the larks singing high up overhead, and the blue sky and bright sun shining steadily and cloud-lessly. That was his most perfect idea of heaven's happiness;

---

[10] *Ibid.*, p. 307.   [11] *Ibid.*, p. 316.

mine was rocking in a rustling green tree, with a west wind blowing, and bright white clouds flitting rapidly above; and not only larks, but throstles, and blackbirds, and . . . close by great swells of long grass undulating in waves to the breeze . . . and the whole world awake and wild with joy. He wanted all to lie in an ecstasy of peace; I wanted all to sparkle, and dance in a glorious jubilee.''[12]

Young Catherine's alternatives were those of her mother, between which she was crushed. In choosing the first, she lost the second, and the second was her heart. The second is, of course, the one Heathcliff would have chosen. Ecstasy is more representative of his nature than tranquillity. For that matter, if one associates joy with tranquillity, and ecstasy with fever, exquisite suffering, and unbearable pleasure, Heathcliff lived his dark and introverted life in contempt of joy. Yet at the end, quite apart from the coincidence of language, the use of "joyful," the concluding scene which Mr. Lockwood leaves with us is in enormous contrast not only with the snowstorm at the start of his tale but with the personality of Heathcliff when alive: "I lingered round them, under that benign sky; watched the moths fluttering among the heath and harebells; listened to the soft wind breathing through the grass; and wondered how anyone could ever imagine unquiet slumbers for the sleepers in that quiet earth.''[13] We are left with tranquillity. Does that mean that the Lintons win out in the end? Or does it mean that even they by facsimile bore the marks of joy which Catherine was drawn to, and which Heathcliff bore in its authentic form in death, in his "frightful lifelike gaze of exaltation."

We are left with questions. Does this story of existential love arise from a young woman's frustrated longing for a lover of her own? And whether it did or not, does a doomed

[12] *Ibid.*, p. 237.   [13] *Ibid.*, p. 320.

love like Heathcliff's and Cathy's suggest a religious or metaphysical search which only God can satisfy beyond the grave? For however one thinks of the union of two bodies in the grave (Abelard and Heloise, Heathcliff and Cathy), it can hardly be compared to their lost union on earth, and it is a pathetic substitute, serving only to confirm the absolute desperation and absolute insistence on a fulfillment in some kind of union. This may be what man seeks, but look what comes his way. To say so much is perhaps to say a great deal, and at least honestly, with no illusions. Maybe there is no more to say, when all is said and done. If so, then even Unamuno's tragic sense of life is a delusion.

Gilson had remarked about Heloise "that the world has never seen her like." This might be said of Heathcliff as well. The world did see Heloise, and for all we know it has seen Heathcliff as well. It has seen him certainly in the dream of a real girl, his creator, Emily Brontë. He, not Cathy, dominates her novel, as in real life it was Heloise who lived frustrated and tormented, not Peter Abelard. The roles are reversed by the difference between real life and the motives of fiction.

14.

THE LANDSCAPE
OF REMEMBERED LOVE

THE world of a man in love has all the characteristics of a foreign country. It has a language of its own. People look different. The frontier is marked and guarded. The customs and attitudes of its people are alien to those of the land from which he came. Life is more intense and more spontaneous. There is no mean, only extremes; anything can happen at any time, and the worst is not death but separation. It can be the loneliest of places to live in, or the most intimate. When it ceases to be either, it is time to go back across the border where only the expected ever happens, and where nothing matters very much except the status quo.

This "country without name" looks different to each person who goes there. No one sees the same towns, hills, valleys, rivers as others he meets there. And when he talks of his favorite landscape, he knows others do not have the same place in mind. And yet they are all there in love. Each crossed the border, probably at different times and at different places, and for different reasons, yet they can all recall in the same words what they have left behind. They can share similar feelings about the uniqueness of the "mysterious country" into which they have wandered. It has become for each of them "a second landscape."

Many people cross over into such a land when they are children, and later they remember it as an oddly distorted replica of a physical and social world which has usually disappeared through the ravages of time, but which, even when it is more or less unchanged, has become for them only an ambience cold and indifferent to their expectations. We expect so much of the past, wanting it to be as it once was, laden with kindness and mystery. But the kindness may have vanished with the parents and friends who were kind, and the mystery is gone because we have grown up and understand all that there ever was to know. Seldom do other landscapes freshly visited make the same impression of welcome and withholding. Therefore, we long regretfully for something we never really had, and in sorrow we find ourselves agreeing with Proust that "the only true Paradise is always the paradise we have lost."[1] It is not necessarily the only paradise, but for many it will always seem so; they will wearily go through the motions of living without affection or hopeful desire, convinced that their future must be as trivial as their present.

Others are made of more resolute material; perhaps they are the fools of our universe. Born to dream—and who is not?—they live out the dream, no matter how broken, to its tragic end. Henri Fournier, known mostly by his pseudonym, Alain-Fournier, was such a man. His childhood landscape was that of the Sologne in central France in the late 1880's and 90's. During all his life, all twenty-eight years of it, this countryside exercised its charm over him in revery and nostalgia. Who knows what he would have made of it if he had not seen a beautiful girl on the steps of the Grand Palais in Paris, on Ascension Day, June 1, 1905. He followed her home, and ten days later, on Whitsunday, accosted her in the street outside the church of St. Germain des Prés, and said, "You are beautiful." After a brief and tentative conversation, she said, "What's the use?" They parted, and only met again eight years later, when she had been married for some years and had two children. In the

---

[1] *The Past Recaptured*, p. 944.

meantime he had placed her in the middle of his nostalgic landscape, and placed both landscape and girl in his novel, *Le Grand Meaulnes*. From 1905 until his death in 1914 the memory of Yvonne de Q. (his Beatrice) preoccupied him.

> You do not know what she was to me. She was like a spirit for ever beside me. I had almost forgotten her face. But I knew she was there, and who she was. I used to take her everywhere, and when she was there, nothing seemed harsh to me any more. I recall a wild and stormy night two years ago, huddled up in the vineyard, when it was such fun, like some entertainment for "us," to be there loving it together. With her love, I used to be superior to everything, yet in love with everything. There was her dignity and my devotion, she had her gracefulness, and I, my strength, and we were quite alone with each other in the middle of the world.[2]

And another time, "On manoeuvres amidst the pink clover on the hills, I suddenly became quite indifferent to all that was not my love, and, for the first time for many months, I looked at her face so fixedly that, for a moment, I thought I could not take another step."[3] We have met this before, in Heathcliff. It is a normal way for the conscious and sub-conscious mind to hang on to a lost love. Probably women carry memories of first loves, lost loves, with them longer than men. But this is not what makes Alain-Fournier's preoccupation out of the ordinary, i.e., not that he was a man, but rather that he projected the nostalgia for his lost love onto the screen of his childhood landscape in a novel which, although obviously autobiographical, surpasses autobiography in its symbolic impression.

If this were not so, we would not even have sympathy for this man who was so sorry for himself. When the caretaker of Yvonne's old house in Paris told him that she had

[2] Jacques Rivière and Alain-Fournier, *Correspondance, 1905–1914* (Paris: Gallimard, 1926), II, 134–35.

[3] *Ibid.*, p. 294.

married, he wrote: " 'Ah, now indeed can I depart. What is left for me here except for you, my friend? I have known for a quarter of an hour now. My pain which I did not feel at first, is getting worse.' "[4] And the next day, "Now I am quite alone with harsh low life. Everything is turning to the pain it used to be. Yesterday, I sensed how much thought of her, even subconsciously, was always a part of me. Yesterday, it seemed that even to walk across the dry yard of the house was a torture for me. She has gone away. I am left alone."[5] Without doubting that this is what he felt—who at twenty-one has not?—it does seem excessive that a young man who met a girl only once, and for a few minutes of unsatisfactory talk, should feel ready for death. And even if we do not accuse him of forced feeling, self-consciously likening himself and the girl, now to Pelléas and Mélisande, now to Tristan and Iseult, we smile over the sorrowful romanticism of schoolboy love. Of such, great literature is not usually made.

As with the Kierkegaardian aesthete, melancholy was his castle, melancholy and an equally Gallic resolve to attain glory. "I am alone. And despite my stifled heart, although I am quite crushed, I must get up again. I need glory. I must win souls. I must rise above it all. . . . My country scenes no longer have their hidden face, mysterious and adorable. My roads no longer lead towards the kingdom of the heart, a kingdom as strange and mysterious as she herself. I have lost those bitter-sweet imaginings she inspired in me, which were all my life. Now I am alone in the centre of the earth."[6] The sentimentalism, the self-pity is thick. It is nevertheless, the ore out of which semi-precious stones are occasionally made. Emily Brontë's

---

[4] Robert Gilson, *The Quest of Alain-Fournier* (New Haven: Yale University Press, 1954), p. 95.

[5] *Correspondance*, II, 134–35.

[6] *Ibid.*

imagination is in better taste. But then she did not have a real love to lose. Real love is usually in part, and often in large part, silly, affected, insincere, and very self-regarding. Who can read Elizabeth Barrett's letters to her future husband without soon choking on the talkativeness of her cherishing? A novelist, like a philosopher, has the immense advantage of not having to report on the high proportion of triviality in the heart of passion. A critic, like a biographer, cannot avoid doing so, and it is just as well. The miracle seems all the more astonishing when it is seen to spring from a pathos which most people would not even make an effort to overcome.

Even here the lover is tempted by convention. And Alain-Fournier was no exception. He too discovered God. "And I weep, obstinately turning my head towards what is forever being snatched from me. And I am left alone and crushed, but still unyielding."[7] But the temptation was strong, to be tempted by the whole bag of tricks. "Something is calling to me desperately, and I am cut off from it by all the roads of the earth.[8]

. . . .

I do not promise you happiness in this world, but in the next. . . . Real joy is not of this world. . . . I beseech you who know me, even if I am never fated to believe, not to consider lightly what I am going to say. For years I have argued with myself, but this time my mind is made up. The day I take that final step, if take it I must, I shall enter orders and become a missionary."[9] Probably others have been led to the jaws of mystical sentiments no more original than these. Disappointment and self-pity are not safe guides. Yet who can say that they are always fallible? For eight years this man luxuriated in his nostalgia for a girl he had never really known. And the last entries in his

[7] *Ibid.*   [8] *Ibid.*, II, 294.   [9] *Ibid.*, II, 301.

notebooks are, if possible, more sentimental than the earlier ones. He had hired an investigator to trace her, and finally he met her sister, and then herself. He even played with her two children at that second meeting. " 'I know now that Yvonne de Galais [his fictional name for her] has two little children. I sobbed through the evening in my room. I am still weeping as I write these words to you. I am suffering terribly . . . I ask myself if I shall be able to go on living.' "[10] He lived another year, until he disappeared in a ground mist somewhere on the Western Front. But the curious thing is that even when he wrote this last entry he had already finished the novel in which the real Yvonne was transformed into Yvonne de Galais, a novel in which he never once overstepped the line between sentiment and sentimentality. In his "Quest for the Girl with the Golden Hair" he had learned to separate the ideal from reality.

Alain-Fournier does not fit into any neat category of the existential or the mystical. His love for the real Yvonne was all along only the starting engine for a quest that no conventional mysticism can define. God came his way as a conventional escape from disappointment in love. He made no effort to explore this way of escape. There is no reason why his novel should be read figuratively as a religious book, unless, of course, one uses the Tillichian language of an "ultimate concern." And I shall not do so. The point is that Alain-Fournier demonstrated that a human being can entertain a profound symbolic search which is both beyond the existential and bypasses the mystical. He knew exactly what he was trying to do, and he wrote it down a year and a half after meeting Yvonne: "I want to express the mystery of the unknown world I long for. And as this world is made of old memories, old

---

[10] Gilson, *The Quest of Alain-Fournier*, p. 202.

unconscious impressions, I want to express the mystery
of those particular impressions the world gives me. But
this task is as huge as life itself. I want to bring my world to
life, the mysterious world I long for, the new and far-off
landscape of my heart. It is of this world both past and
still desired, mysteriously mingled with the world of my
life, mysteriously suggested by it, that I wish to speak.[11]
Except for one thing, this could define the existential world
of Heloise or Heathcliff. He longed for the unknown as
well as the known. Without realizing it, he had surpassed
Yvonne de Q. almost as soon as he had met her. It could
be argued that he was experiencing the beginning of a
truly mystical longing. Perhaps he was. It could also be
argued that if he had married Yvonne de Q. their very
happiness together might have been founded on just such
a vision of their own future. They would enter that mysterious country together. As it turned out, what was not
possible in marriage took place in art. And who is to say
for sure which is the more difficult or which the more
satisfying?

A schoolboy, Augustin Meaulnes, gets lost in the fields
away from home one night. He dreams of a young girl
sitting with her back to him as he wakes from a deep sleep.
He does not have strength enough to get out of bed "in
this enchanted dwelling." The next day he wanders on and
comes upon an old manor in the forest decorated for a
wedding. Everybody has been invited, and he is no more a
stranger than the rest. "He had dropped into the most
peaceful happiness on earth." All are waiting for the
bridegroom to appear with his bride. As they all wait,
Meaulnes sees the bride, Frantz de Galais' sister Yvonne.
The look she gives him seems to say, "I don't know you.
And yet it seems to me that I do know you." He follows

[11] *Correspondance*, I, 415–16.

her and says, "You are beautiful." He asks to be forgiven for annoying her; she replies, "I forgive you." They
talk a little more as they walk about the grounds. Finally
she says, "What's the use?" as the real Yvonne de Q.
had, but adds, as the real Yvonne had not, "I will wait for
you."

This mixture of wish and reality forms the texture of the
novel. Fournier's real vision had been kept alive not only
by the dream of seeing Yvonne de Q. again but by a dream
of life as a "mysterious land" of beauty and peace, of
which the Sologne and Yvonne were figures. It is no
accident, I am sure, that he named his errant young hero
Augustin. For, as in Fournier's own life, so Augustin
Meaulnes kept the vision in his heart but lost his way
back to the girl and the "sand-pit manor." He and his
schoolboy friend, François Seurel, who tells the story, try
without success to find the lost land and "the most beautiful girl the world may ever have held." Augustin leaves
school, seeking her in the city. Someone tells him that she
has married. In despair he takes up with a girl who is the
fiancée that Yvonne's brother was to have brought with
him to the sand-pit manor for their wedding. Unknowingly
he betrays Yvonne and her brother. Some time later Seurel,
by chance, discovers where the lost land is. He takes Meaulnes there and meets Yvonne again: they marry. But the
day after the wedding Meaulnes leaves her in order to
redeem himself in his own eyes by bringing together
Frantz de Galais and his fiancée. He finds them and brings
them home a year after Yvonne has died in childbirth.

It is a simple, affecting story, even without our knowing
that it covers and controls a real encounter and a real quest.
What immediately turns it into something more than a
cover for autobiography is its deliberate use of the symbolism of the sleeping beauty fairy tale. An enchanted

158

wood with turret and spire showing over the trees, the long driveway, the bustling crowd of children and peasants in the courtyard, the lovely girl—it is a vision to match the dream of the lost and tired Meaulnes. But when he wakes, back at school, it is the girl and the castle who are lost. Life then becomes an adventure, at the end of which is not happiness but tragedy. "The adventure that failed," "the happiness that failed," "the lost happiness" constitute the reverse of the ending of the old fairy tale. And it is this reversal that distinguishes Alain-Fournier's symbolic understanding of life.

He knew what he had missed, the premonitory discovery of Meaulnes as he walks up the drive toward the manor. "A strange contentment urged him on, a perfect and almost intoxicating peace, the assurance that his goal had been reached and that he had now nothing but happiness to expect." His summary, "so much joy," reinforces the observation that what Alain-Fournier remembered and looked for was not ecstasy but joy, not frenzied sexual union but "a secret understanding which death alone was to break and a friendship more moving than a great passion." Of course, we know that he never achieved this. But this vision was what made life worth living. There is nothing more moving than the suppressed love of young Seurel finding the surface. Meaulnes' adventures, Meaulnes' quest, become Seurel's. And after Meaulnes leaves his young wife, Seurel watches over her. The day after she dies he alone is there to mourn, and as he fights "against hideous revolt and a blinding flood of tears" he says to himself: "We had again found the beautiful girl. We had won her. She was my friend's wife and I myself had loved her with that deep secret friendship that is never told." Alain-Fournier had learned to control his own self-pity, by giving one part of himself to Meaulnes, one part to Seurel, by letting the non-lover express love.

The thematic movement of the novel takes the reader from dream and encounter to tragedy and death. In between is the nostalgic search for "the lost path to the lost paradise," or in Proustian terms, "lost time." The two quests, Proust's and Fournier's, were being conducted simultaneously. Fournier's question, "Can the past come to life?" was not Proust's. He knew it could not, and he did not waste new time hoping for the return of old time. Fournier used up eight years of his life—at least on one plane of those eight years—actively looking for the Yvonne he met on Whitsunday, 1905. And every year, on this Pentecostal feast, he observed the anniversary. He did not want to find a way of remembering her as if she were present; that was Proust's way. He wanted to find *her*, speak to *her* again. He could not believe, even eight years later, that "God has shown me so much, promised me so much, and will give me nothing—in this world, or in the next." His problem was not psychological, it was metaphysical. "Can the past come to life?" Can you ever return? And if you do, will it be the same again? Proust discovered, and the discovery was profound and important, that nostalgic return restores psychological presence. But Henri Fournier did not need to discover this; he carried her presence around with him all the time. Like Heathcliff, he wanted the real Yvonne, not a feeling of her presence. And when they finally met, he realized that there was no return, only a second meeting. He could not say, "We have returned and begun again." It is possible that her married happiness was not the only barrier on that day; it might also have been the same sense of betrayal that embittered Meaulnes before he found Yvonne de Galais again, so embittered him that he said, "I have renounced paradise."

160

Proust could document the changes of time itself that make returns impossible. Fournier understood something further, the changes in ourselves. For this reason, and on this point, there is more to learn from him. In a time like ours, when spiritual quests are rather pushed aside by the clamor of public events and technological achievement, it is also necessary that someone remind us of "the lost path" to "the lost paradise." Alain-Fournier's conscious effort to retain, for the sake of intellectual continuity, the symbolism of the sleeping beauty, should not be forgotten. It could be ours. " 'I am searching for something far more mysterious. It is the path told of in books, the ancient obstructed path, the path to which the weary prince could find no entrance. It is found at last at the most forlorn hour of the morning, when you have long since forgotten that eleven or twelve is about to strike. . . . And suddenly, as one thrusts aside bushes and brier, with a movement of hesitating hands unevenly raised level to the face, it appears in sight as a long shadowy avenue, the outlet of which is a small round patch of light.' "[12] The heading of this chapter, "A la recherche du sentier perdu," could have been the title of the whole book. The book itself is the way to Fournier's own lost land. He had not really lost a person, for he had never owned Yvonne, never even known her. He had not lost the Sologne or some other beloved section of central France; he could return there at any time. But he had lost the power to see the world through the eyes of a child. " 'I am convinced, now, that when I discovered the nameless manor, I was at the height of what stands for perfection and pure motive in any one's heart, a height I shall never reach again. In death alone, as I once wrote to you, I may hope to find again the beauty of that day.' "[13]

[12] Alain-Fournier, *The Wanderer*, trans. Françoise Delisle (New York: Doubleday Anchor, 1953), pp. 138–39.
[13] *Ibid.*, p. 184.

"Whosoever shall not receive the kingdom of God as a little child, he shall not enter therein."[14] And Meaulnes did not enter. Yvonne was dead when he finally came home. The friend, not the husband, had remained loyal to "the beauty of that day." But even the friend, when he carried the body of Yvonne down the narrow stairway, the dead hair straying into his mouth, was left with "the taste of earth and death." Meaulnes returned home only to go off once more for "new adventures." Who is left to remember what it had all meant? It is as if Alain-Fournier, speaking for Henri Fournier, were asking himself, "Can anything of my dream survive death?" And his answer (or was it only another question?) was, "Yes, in the heart of François Seurel." It is only at some remove that beauty—"perfection and pure motive"—is stronger than death.

Existential beauty fades and finally crumbles into dust. Mystical beauty is an abstraction good only for those who do not know existential beauty. It can set the heart aching unendurably for what it cannot have. No torment can exceed the torment of the woman enclosed in a convent with the memory of a lost love still outside. She cannot pretend to love God when what she really wants is a man. What authority, in any case, does she have to turn away from her "neighbor" for the sake of God alone? Too many lives have been twisted into a lie in order to avoid thinking of a lost love, or a love that has not yet come. How can the real God, not the notional God of Manichean saints, be worshiped apart from the real world? God is usually an abstraction rather than a mystery. St. Augustine sometimes understood this, although usually he was one of the angriest defenders of the wall between existential and mystical. In his commentary on the Fourth Gospel he said, "The love of God comes first in the order of enjoining, but the

---

[14] St. Mark 10:15.

162

love of our neighbor first in the order of doing. . . . Because thou dost not yet see God, thou dost earn the seeing of God. . . . Love, therefore, thy neighbor; and behold that in thee whereby thou lovest thy neighbor; there wilt thou see, as thou mayest, God."[15] And one day while preaching he pointed to the Sacrament on the altar and said to the congregation, "If you are the Body of Christ and His members, then that which is on the altar is the mystery of yourselves; receive the mystery of yourselves." We might speak in the same manner of the relationship between existential and mystical. God is the mystery of ourselves, and of all the rest of creation. This may not exhaust God, but it exhausts us. What experience of God can a man have except through the created world and its created thoughts? We do well to remember that there is a difference between our thoughts and God's, between real creation and our image which we like to call creative. If we touch God only in creation, the most dangerous blasphemy is to identify our theological abstractions of divinity with the real mystery.

No one knew better than Charles Williams what that mystery is. His command was, "Adore the mystery of love." If only we could, But often there does not seem to be enough to go round between men and women, between parents and children, between rich and poor, between nations. Or, to use Simone Weil's better word, it may be there, but we have not "consented" to use it. Sometimes it seems that men love their neighbors, far and near, without loving God. There is less to worry about in this than in loving God without loving one's neighbor. Simone Weil's suggestion that we think of this as an implicit love of God may lead some men back to the Pauline symbolism of the body of Christ. If they are really God's body, how

---

[15] In Joan. Evang., XVII, 8, *An Augustine Synthesis*, p. 353.

can they not be adoring God when they adore the members of the body? How could they miss Him? And where would they find him, still in their bodies, if they sought him outside? "I went out of myself in the search for You, and did not find the God of my heart." Perhaps St. Augustine did not have this in mind; his ambivalent (he lusted and he feared) attitude toward sex prevented him from seeing the full implications of the Pauline imagery. Only now are any Christians emancipated enough from his creeping Manicheism to believe not only that matter was redeemed as well as honored by the Incarnation, but that the God who once appeared in history still appears to man in human existence. It might seem unnecessary to say this, yet it must be said again just because the obvious has gone unnoticed for so long. The Christian has traditionally (in his praying) conceived God as separated from matter because He is spirit. Now in an age when prayer has become almost impossible for many who still want to be Christians, we may be driven to reappraise the intellectualizing side of prayer that has set up an abstraction totally separate from the actual matter and energy of the world. It is the mystery of matter and energy that men should be worshiping, not mystery in and by itself. God does not ask men to love Him alone—in spite of what celibates and virgins have said—but to love him in loving their neighbor. No one has so distorted the implications of the Incarnation as the saints themselves. Christianity badly needs new kinds of saints, not enclosed puritans, but men and women like Jesus who stay in and with the world to the end, and, if possible, beyond.

We should be able to sympathize with the peculiar obstinacy of Simone Weil who loved Christ and the Church, but loved the world too much to leave it. She had been taught a Christianity that required separation of

164

the existential as she knew it (men and women not in the
Church) from the mystical (at least the institution which
claimed to represent it). She knew something was wrong
with this dualism, but did not have time or patience to
find out. The Church had taught her all she knew of
Christ, and yet the Church seemed to her to be asking her
to separate herself from most of mankind and join an
exclusive club. That made no sense, and she refused. No
one should suppose her obstinacy did not make her suffer.
Her dilemma and her suffering can be heard in all its
pathos in the last pages of her *Notebooks*.[16]

There she imagined a man coming to her, telling her she
knew nothing, and asking her to follow him. She did, and
was taken to a church where a priest ordered her to kneel
"in love, as before the place where lies the truth." He took
her to a garret where they were alone. They ate bread, and
drank wine. "This bread really had the taste of bread. I
have never found that taste again." She expected him to
teach her, but they only talked, as friends do, of one thing
and another. One day he said, "Now go." She begged him
not to drive her off, but he threw her out. She never even
tried to find the place again. "I understood that he had
come for me by mistake. My place is not in that garret.
It can be anywhere—in a prison cell, in one of those middle-
class drawing-rooms full of knick-knacks and red plush,
in the waiting room of a station."

Then there follow the two short paragraphs that tell the
secret of her life: "Sometimes I cannot help trying, fear-
fully and remorsefully to repeat to myself a part of what
he said to me. How am I to know if I remember rightly?
He is not there to tell me. . . . I know well that he does not
love me. How could he love me? And yet deep down within me something, a particle of myself, cannot help thinking,

[16] II, 638–39.

with fear and trembling, that perhaps, in spite of all, he loves me." The garret, the Church, was not for her, even though she had been taken there by Christ. The waiting room was more suitable; she could wait for God there. She could not remember for sure all she had been told. Who is there to tell her in His absence? In any case, she could not believe that she had ever been loved. And could she be sure even of that?

In Malory's story of Launcelot and Gwynevere, courtly humility is sometimes rewarded. Heloise also extracted crumbs of compassion, if not affection, from Abelard. She knew she had been loved. All Simone Weil could remember was that she had been spoken to. Of her it might be said: "She spoke because he first spoke to her." But she loved too. The reason for her death proves that. During the war, when she was ill in England, she refused to eat in order to express in the only way she had left her sympathy with those in occupied France who were starving. Should we not say for her that she loved because He first loved her? She had chosen to identify herself with those who had not heard Christ speak. Should we not say that she did so because she had heard Him speak to her?

Simone Weil is a symbol, one more to consider and learn from. She may not have meant to be, any more than Henri Fournier intended to edify anyone else. They and the writer of the Song of Songs, St. John of the Cross, and Emily Brontë have left symbols of themselves and their vision of the mystery of love. Each is different, yet in constellation they can illuminate our lives. Very few men in history are destined to do so much. The rest of us would do well to try to assimilate their dreams into our own range of love. There is no time left to hesitate, and the time has gone when we can be satisfied with either/or's that force us to exclude. Experience is one. The mystical is always somewhere within the existential.

IV

15.

AN IDEA OF LOVE

*When I am dead, tell the kingdom of earth that
I have loved it more than I ever dared to say.*
— Bernanos

THE ROOT of all evils is frustration of love. And in the
name of love it is blasphemous to repress the existential for the sake of the mystical, or the mystical for the
sake of the existential. The skeptic feels safer when he
ignores mystery. The contemplative feels safer when he
hides from matter. Each must exclude and repress to find
tranquillity. It can be done, at a cost. Whether it is worth
doing is another thing. I myself have chosen the fullness
as well as the risks implied in the maxim, "Nothing is to
be excluded." And I have concluded that "The mystical
is within the existential."

Perhaps this is about all that one should try to defend.
Yet there is always more to be said. There still remains the
most practical question of all, "What should one look
for in love?" And if one assumes that to live is to love,
"What kind of love is worth living for?" It is disconcerting,
to say the least, to have settled the dialectical question of
the polarity of existential and mystical only to find that the
lineaments of love's face are scattered, not gathered in
memorable concentration. To gather the criteria of love is
to discover a kind of Platonic "idea" of love.

The life lived from day to day hardly helps. Its triviality
and its false emotions suffocate desire along with responsiveness. Personal experience, even when intense,
needs perspectives from art and history. Poets on the one

169

hand and contemplatives on the other can guarantee the survival, if not the flowering, of something purer than ourselves in ourselves. The ardor and the clarity of vision in someone else often rescues from oblivion the symbolic treasures of nostalgia and desire, reminders that love is as strong as death.

Help can come from odd places. Mystical love sometimes learns from the existential, and existential from the mystical. One of those on whom St. Thomas Aquinas called for an insight into the nature of contemplation, Richard of St. Victor, had elementary things to teach more important than the more abstract schema that interested St. Thomas. The latter, preoccupied with an almost twentieth-century phenomenological inquiry into the motions of a soul in contemplation, drew on Richard's better-known treatises, *Benjamin Minor* and *Benjamin Major*, rather than on his essay, "Four Stages of Passionate Love."[1] Had there been more passion in St. Thomas himself, he might have discovered for us some of the complexities of human longing that have been left for us now to unravel. Richard at least begins with an admirable and Augustinian personal directness: "Love urges me to speak." It hardly matters what kind of love he had in mind, he has said the first thing first: the cause and the topic are one and the same. And if Richard knew only love for God, then his testimony is all the more important on behalf of this fundamental stirring of the soul which we call love. It is interchangeable, now existential, now mystical.

Like St. Bernard, his contemporary, he calls upon the Song of Songs for illustration, but unlike St. Bernard his analysis of love is humanly plausible. For the orthodox

[1] Richard of St. Victor, *Selected Writings on Contemplation*, trans. Clare Kirchberger (London: Faber, 1957).

answer one went to St. Bernard, and if one did not go (as Abelard and Heloise did not) he went to them. We can all learn from Richard of St. Victor. He has a common touch. Like anyone in love he wants to talk about love, and because he is a philosopher he manages to give some order to his experience. He says that we first experience love as a "wound," yet we cannot, perhaps do not want to, hide the hurt, the burning of desire. St. John of the Cross later used this image; it was Richard's first. Some wounds only hurt; the wounding by violent desire exposes all that is usually kept private and out of sight. Inside the soul all is compulsive, self-absorbed, obsessed. St. Maria Maddalena could think only of God, Heloise only of Abelard. Richard goes on to say that passion "binds." No wonder that everyone, including quite often the lover himself, says that the man in love is "sick" (*amore langueo*). For Richard a sick man is one who needs the one thing he cannot have, love; and nothing but love will satisfy his distress. He will just "faint" away (languish, to use the English of *langueo*). Richard had, however, the characteristic orthodox hope—prejudice—that human love cannot satisfy human love, and this is why he concluded his four stages by insisting that not only can the lover not be put off by lesser satisfactions—money, a good job, friends, and so on—he will not even be satisfied by the response he thought he was looking for. There is all too much truth in this. So many lovers—of man, of God—are let down in the anticipated fulfillment they had hopelessly desired and dreamed of. "Is this all it amounts to?" Richard adds, piously, that only God can cure this insatiable and wholly desperate illness. We may add, "And he does not always choose to."

Richard's analysis of desire forces one to do the same for love, assuming the difference between them as between

171

longing and fulfillment. How is love to be known when it appears? What is its role in the rest of life? Love begins, when powerful, as passion and dream, and, if not thwarted, marches toward a fidelity beyond union as well as dream. There may be three, four, seven, nine stages along the way—the number depends on evidence largely personal—but the way leads to an emotional and intellectual plateau where the final landscape can be taken in at leisure. "So here we are—so this is love—now we can live." But before one arrives he must believe in the supremacy of love; without it life is not worth living. And with it evil can be borne. Some do think love the highest, and yet fear it cannot last. They may not wish to commit themselves, for fear of disillusion. They will never reach the plateau at all. Love reveals herself only to those who trust her as much as they desire her. This takes courage in a world that is openly hostile to both adoration and compassion. The first test of love is its ability to live in darkness, without encouragement, if not "despised and rejected of men." The second test is its vision, the idea of love that has sustained the soul in darkness and been confirmed in the light.

It is safe to assume that love fulfilled must match longing, depth for depth, intensity for intensity. St. John of the Cross was moved by the line from the street song, "I am dying of love, dearest, what shall I do?" The reply was, "Die!" It might as well have been, "Live!" And so a man may sometimes feel so much love inside him that he does not know what to do with it all. This is his intensity of desire, whether to touch or to possess or to worship. Love that does not swell to the pressure point of explosion is not a final love, but something preparatory, less intense and sometimes less innocent.

Love that yearns without expectation is unhappy, frustrated of its natural end. This is how we distinguish between desire and love. But lovers often live in an expectation of rebuff that is worse than the sterility of non-transitive desire. Their misery, the product of memory and fear, can give a different meaning to St. Maria Maddalena's "no more love, no more love!" There can be nothing worse than love if all it brings is fear. A happy lover, on the other hand, should be able to wake up in the morning and say, "I know it will be a good day, because I shall be with so and so [man or God]." He is confident that he lives in a world where he will not have the rug pulled from under him and is therefore free to love—not because he is loved in return but because love is permitted in this dark world.

And so the question of the meaning of life is assured, settled once for all. We can say, with Lady Julian of Norwich, "Love was his meaning."[2] We do not need to keep asking, "What is it all about?" We know. It is doing this, loving, and then doing whatever love allows. And when anyone says, "Tell me, now," "Show me what . . .," we can reply just by pointing: "See, there is my love, look at what I am now doing, this is what I mean." For this is what is hidden in the question, "What is the meaning of life?" What can we *do*—not what can we *think*—that will make all the difference? What can be done to resolve the embittered loneliness of one who "cannot emerge from himself" (Proust)? Love is the means of the emerging; love is therefore the meaning.

When meaning is assured, death no longer matters in the same hopeless way. Not only because "people go on loving without seeing each other," as Graham Greene put it, but because "love is as strong as death," and not dependent on life. This conviction arises out of a discovery of the supremacy of responsive love. And this is why some lovers are

[2] *Revelations of Divine Love*, p. 202.

able to endure the loss of each other without suffering incurable despair. For grief which is love's registration of loss can be transformed by the lost love into gratitude for having been given so much love. Likewise the dread of death that springs from the knowledge that life has been so far wasted will largely dissipate once love is fulfilled. And if the lover left behind does not yet live with the clear consolation of hope, he will at least have the comfort of a realized longing—and that is a good deal.

But to be realized, the longing must be acknowledged, at least with some degree of sympathy. Love at a distance can never be happy enough to be called anything but love on the way: it is wish, not fact. Most lovers want their love returned; only the most humble do not dare even to wish for a response. Only a rare few settle for permission merely to love, to please, and to serve. But these few understand from the heart what the others must learn from hard experience, that both adoration and compassion are absolutely free gifts, sacrificial in nature. "We love because he first loved us." And that love was sacrificial by intention, a pure oblation. The lover who so distorts love into becoming a desire for possession never finds out the joy of a selfless offering that looks forward to a response so that it will have an additional reason to be grateful.

Like everything else love is surrounded by the misconceptions and distortions of our frail nature. Many suppose that familiarity can deflate love as it deflates all else. The fact that so many married couples, so many unmarried couples, bore each other, is not proof of the risk of overexposure, but of a failure in loving. On the contrary, the more that true lovers see one another, the deeper their love should be. Whether like St. Maria Maddalena or like Heloise, they can hardly keep eyes, minds, or hands off each other. Daily they learn more and more about each

174

other and, surprisingly, about the world of their new common vision.

Love has enlarged their vision and increased their will to work. The world becomes once more the friendly world of a protected childhood, warm, exciting, plastic. Secure in affection, lovers can afford to relax, and to tolerate in donated tranquillity much that used to threaten and jar. Indeed, there may be a risk of losing some discrimination or resolution, if the tranquillity allows any return to dreaming. The more secure in love, the easier it is to confess that the two great loves, existential and mystical, are equally valid. The more intensely the loved one is worshiped, the greater the chance that adoration will develop a new branch, compassion. A passion for justice not only may follow a passion for persons, it is its only reliable test. "Whoever has done it unto one of the least of these my brethren has done it unto me."

Just as a good love includes all things, many and contrary, so a good love can unify the interior life of man. While waiting for this unity the soul finds its hoped-for identity in moments of nostalgia, with its promise and taste of presence. In real life and real presence the unity of scattered past and wished-for presence is encountered in intuitions of ordered simplicity. Recurrent dream sequences in the night, typical personal symbols and memories in the daytime, once tantalizing and frustrating, now turn out to be figures in a unique interior landscape all our own. Love has done this too.

It can do more. In shared experience man and God, man and woman, reach out through the whole world, beyond possessiveness and disappointment, toward the mystery of their brief lives. What once seemed incomprehensible, dark and chill, now seems familiar and accepting. To love is to journey backward into the mystery of the earthly paradise where God is still an occasional visitor. He is no longer the only master; we have been taught by life itself during the long exile. We were spirit crying for matter, soul crying for body. We had needed someone to lift from us the weight and the ache of unfulfilled longing. That is why love, whether existential or mystical, has to be imagined and expressed sacramentally. We take it in our hands. We are made for love: it is our first vocation. When men and women finally dare to confess—are able to confess—that they, like Mary Magdalene, have loved much, it is almost time for them to die. There is no better time. At least they are ready for whatever is yet to come, in life or death. A new freedom has been won, a perfect balance—not a tension—between discipline and passion, knowing and pleasing. It no longer matters whether love is called existential or mystical. The two great loves are at last in real accord.

176

INDEX OF NAMES

Human Love—Existential and Mystical

by Ralph Harper

designer: Edward King
typesetter: Baltimore Type and Composition Corporation
typefaces: Garamond (text) and Deepdene (display)
printer: J. H. Furst Company
paper: Warren's Olde Style
binder: Moore & Co., Inc.
cover material: Holliston Payko